THE AFTERLIFE OF PLAYS

Jonathan Miller

Fifth Distinguished Graduate
Research Lecture
San Diego State University

Graduate Division and Research

SAN DIEGO STATE UNIVERSITY PRESS

ISBN 1-879691-12-4 (cloth)

Published by
San Diego State University Press

San Diego State University
San Diego, CA 92182

CONTENTS

The Distinguished Graduate Research Lecture Series

The Distinguished Graduate Research Lecture Series of San Diego State University brings eminent scientists and scholars of national and international status to the campus to present all-university graduate colloquia on generic problems of research and graduate education. These colloquia combine open lectures of general interest with smaller seminars and workshops for the graduate students and faculty who are actively pursuing research in areas related to the colloquia topics. The series is sponsored by the Graduate Division and Research and the University Research Council and is supported in part through Instructionally Related Activities Funds. Each academic discipline or department which offers a graduate degree at San Diego State University may nominate notable scholars to participate in the series. Exposure to and interaction with such distinguished researchers is an integral part of the instructional experience for all graduate students at San Diego State University. Each of the lectures in the series will be published to assure their increased availability to the students and faculty of the university and to the community at large. This book, *The Afterlife of Plays*, originated as San Diego State University's Fifth Distinguished Graduate Research Lecture.

1 *COLLOQUIUM*

Dean Feinberg:
Good morning. I'm Larry Feinberg, and on behalf of the Graduate Division and Research and the University Research Council, I'm very delighted to welcome you all to this morning's colloquium with Dr. Jonathan Miller. I think many of you know that this morning's colloquium is one of a number of events that are scheduled in conjunction with our Distinguished Graduate Research Lecture which Dr. Miller will be delivering this afternoon at 4:00 p.m. in Montezuma Hall. The title of his lecture is "The Afterlife of Plays." This morning's colloquium provides an opportunity for faculty and graduate students and guests of the community to interact with Dr. Miller on a somewhat more informal basis than could be possible at the lecture. It also gives us a chance to explore a whole other realm of Dr. Miller's interests and expertise. At this point I would like to turn the proceedings over to Dr. Robert Kaplan, professor of psychology, and Dr. Kevin Patrick, who is the director of our health services, who will introduce our guest and engage Dr. Miller in a conversation on medicine. Bob . . .

Professor Kaplan:
Thank you. It's a great pleasure to be here today to introduce Dr. Jonathan Miller. Dr. Miller is an author, a lecturer, and television producer and has had his productions in a variety of different media including opera, film, and the stage. Dr. Miller received his early education at St. Paul's School, and from there he went to St. John's College at Cambridge University, where he qualified as a doctor of medicine in 1959. Within the theatre he has produced a wide variety of Shakespearean plays, including the *Merchant of Venice* and many others. His non-Shakespearean productions include Chekhov's *The Three Sisters* and *The Seagull*, Eugene O'Neill's *Long Days Journey into Night*, which was produced both in New York and in London with Jack Lemmon. He is currently doing *The Taming of the Shrew* for the Royal Shakespeare Theatre. In 1988 he will be the artistic director for Old Vic.

Within the opera he has performed and produced a variety of operas, which have been staged in Australia, Germany, England, and the United States, to name just a few. Some of the productions include *Arden Must Die*, *Orpheo*, *Don Giovanni*, *The Magic Flute*, and *Tosca*. As many of you know from reading the papers, he's currently doing *Tristan* in Los Angeles with Zubin Mehta.

In television he's done *The Body in Question*, which was a series for the BBC covering the history of medicine. In 1980 and 1981, he produced twelve Shakespearean plays for the BBC. In 1985 and 1986, he produced Mozart's *Cosi Fan Tutte*, an extension of the production he had done in St. Louis. Some of his books include *The Body in Question*, *States of Mind*, and some interesting pop-up books on the human body and facts of life.

It's really a great pleasure to have Dr. Miller with us. He has mentioned that he would rather be called Jonathan. Also joining us today is Dr. Kevin Patrick, who is our director of health services. Dr. Miller has mentioned to us that he would like the audience to participate, so those of you who feel you would like to be up here with us, if you have questions we would be happy to entertain them. To lead off today Dr. Patrick has the first question.

Dr. Patrick:
Thanks, Bob. A question pertaining to bedside manner. I know you talked about this, and it's an appropriate subject for a medical intro. Norman Cousins has stated that medical students typically arrive at medical school in a state of what he calls educational disequilibrium. They have emphasized, much to their detriment, science over the humanities. They have had little training in human behaviors. Would you care to comment on this, and if you could design a medical educational process, how would you do that in ways that would perhaps deal with this problem?

Dr. Miller:
It's very easy to start designing medical programs from a distance when you haven't really got to make it stick, so that most of the ideas that I might have are sort of utopian transfers, really. I do think there are problems about people coming into medicine the way that they do, perhaps because they're trained in science first. I'm not certain that a training in the humanities actually makes them into better doctors. I think that reading *Middlemarch* doesn't actually make you into a better person, and science may not actually preempt the possibility of being a sympathetic person either. I actually think the problem is that you get people too young, not that they're ignorant by being scientists, but probably people start too young. I know that they start later in the United States and that they have to be graduates before they can become MDs. Even so, I think probably it's too early. I wouldn't let anyone really lay hands on patients until they were 30. I just think that the most important experience you have to have is just simply living life. I don't think a course in the humanities necessarily helps you. I think there's a prevailing belief, perhaps stronger in the United States than it is in

England, that you could actually legislate for improvements in personality. You could just set up ideal conditions to make people warm, relating, nice people who would be naturally good at the bedside.

I remember once seeing an example of this when I was doing that opera you mentioned, *Cosi Fan Tutte*, in St. Louis. I went to Barnes Hospital on a grand round on the maximum patients' surgical floor where people were suffering and undergoing really the most appalling and mutilative operations for carcinomas of the upper respiratory tract. There were also problems with the young interns and the young residents having to confront these things. There were plans to have psychiatric sessions for benefit of the residents and the interns. I really found myself objecting very much to the scheme. It seemed to me to be typical of what I think is happening today, that you can actually set up programs to fix things to get people to be less disturbed by or more responsive to, say, mutilating operations. I don't think it's a matter of psychiatry. It's actually a matter of encouraging the imagination in some ways, and that's not necessarily done best by expert systems. I would dread having a psychiatrist tell me how to adjust myself to the idea that half of someone's face was going to be taken away. I think that the way you do this is by using plain English very clearly and saying, "What you're going to see is someone with half of their face not there. Try and imagine what it's like having a skin graft which results in your nipple growing out of your tongue." This is what I saw in the ward there. But instead there are these elaborate, expert-system circumlocutions to remove, which are supposed to actually train these kids into sensitive human beings. Actually, I don't think there is any way of legislating for it. I don't think programs in humanities do it either. You can read *Middlemarch* until you are blue in the face, but I don't think you'll do better at the bedside. I think actually what does make people better at the bedside is just simply living out some other form of existence before you are allowed the privilege of laying hands on someone else's body. I think people come to it too early. I just think that a whippersnapper of twenty-two who is allowed to ask someone whether their sex life is very good . . . it's an impudence. I think that these are intimate questions. I think people ought to be qualified to ask people the questions. It's a great privilege to have access to someone else's body and someone else's privacy, and I don't like the idea of a young punk being allowed to do that simply because he's wearing a white coat. We robe people in white coats and stethoscopes and give them reins of office. This licenses them to intrude in ways in which we normally would hit them in the face for asking such questions if they weren't wearing white coats. I really think that we ought to start later.

Dr. Patrick:
Did you feel this way when you finished your training?

Dr. Miller:
Yes, I did. I felt I got there too early. I was at sea. I was a good scientific student. I

had been taught all about membrane physiology, and I knew all about that and was quite good at it, but I was really at sea in conversations with patients. When I look back at it, I don't know how I dared to ask some of the older people some of the questions I did, and I blush with shame at my impudence now. It makes it sound as if I am encouraging the idea of some entirely geriatric medical service. Believe me, I am not at peace with asking young people intimate questions either. I wish it could strike some happy medium; that's all.

Lengthening the university course is not the answer. Lengthening the university course simply extends the telescopic tube insulation so that people have even less chance of encountering real life.

Professor Kaplan:
In *The Body in Question*, there is an interesting portion where you hint that the arts and scientific thought run parallel. For instance, you suggest that Galen came along at a time when the arts were very descriptive. If that's so, where are we now?

Dr. Miller:
When I made that point in *The Body in Question*, I was really saying that there are certain parallels I didn't really want to pursue too closely. I do think that scientific thought has many features in common with various artistic enterprises. There is a much higher degree of conjectural imagination involved than some scientists would like to admit—part of the publicity manifesto of science, a very old-fashioned idea, but it is inductive, and it actually proceeds by gathering data. Then you get a theory out of it. We all know that that's not how it happens. It's a hypothetical deductive system. We project hypotheses often far beyond what the data allow, and that's rather like the arts. It's metaphoric. It involves huge metaphoric leaps of imagination, and that's how you tell you are in the presence of a good scientist. It also has to be checked by experiment and so forth. In that sense they are related to one another.

The timing of certain things that occur in science with a return to a pleasure-taking and physical reality is certainly, I think, true with the growth of physical realism in painting in the 15th century, which coincides with the growth of an interest in human anatomy. There was, as it were, a reaction against that sort of metaphysical soulfulness which overtook Western Europe after the fall of the Western Roman Empire. Now what's happening is extremely hard to say, but science has become something which it never was before. It's a giant megalopolis. It's an enormous institution. Nothing like that ever existed. Even the word "scientist" is very new. It only existed, after all, from the 1840s, coined, I think, by Whewell, the English philosopher of science. Then, you see, scientists were simply scattered amateurs, really. It took them quite a long time to establish institutions and universities. Now you have these giant institutions. At the neuroscience annual meeting, one of the big international conferences in neuroscience which was held this year, at Denver or somewhere, I think there were 22,000 people there. Sherrington, at the beginning of the century, would have been astounded at the idea of there being 22,000. The 22,000 was simply, as it were, the plankton of the subject. There are the sedentary scientists still attached to their base who haven't travelled at all, so that if you think of this vast institution, it is terribly hard to make any comments about what the state of science is now except that, in a way, its social character is almost as important as its cognitive character. Its cognitive character varies so much from science to science that I wouldn't be prepared to say too much about it. There's only one thing that I would say very briefly, which, I think overlaps with the arts; that is, that science is generating images at a rate which it never did before, as a sort of visual exhaust out the back of the system. It's chucking out an enormous number of images which are part of its normal currency used inside the community but doing its business. You think a computer generates images of this and that. I mean I can hardly enumerate the types of visual images which are now being created, but actually what happens is that this exhaust is being thrown out the back of the machine and being picked up by artists and exploited for decorative visual purposes, which, in fact are, in many ways appalling to the scientists. They say, well, this is technical stuff, and you are just simply misusing it. It has got no relationship to what's going on in the arts—the visual arts—at all.

Professor Kaplan:
Can you tell us a little bit more about the social character of science? What do you mean by that?

Dr. Miller:
What I mean by it really has to do with the fact that it is a vast institution, the fact that it is funded. You see, when someone like Michael Foster, for example, started physiology school in the 1870s in Cambridge, there was no public funding of science. The whole business of science wasn't a business of science until then. In 1830 in England, when people like Brewster and Babbage (the calculating-machine man) wrote, there was a great controversy which was carried on in the quarterly magazines in the 1830s in which Babbage and Brewster complained about the state of English science in comparison to its state on the continent. They complained it was amateurish, that the Royal Society was itself a shambles, and it was filled with all sorts of amateurs and anecdotal clergymen who would send in occasional accounts of a thunderstorm or peculiar object that they'd found on the beach or this or that place. It was quite clear that it was an amateurish subject, and it is different now. It is a vast, professional, subsidized, funded megalopolis with, above all, something that which had never happened before, a huge intellectual proletariat. That sounds like a cruel thing to say at a university, but everyone knows what I'm talking about. When you get an institution of that size, there are people slaving away in the vineyards of it who are never going to become famous, important, or anything, but the whole business of science depends on their activity. There are post-docs and people who are barely

hanging on to tenure who are going to be slaving away doing that for the rest of their lives. Without it science will collapse, and this is one of the great tragedies of it. I think one of the things we are going to see is enormous social restlessness inside this scientific megalopolis. That's the thing which I find, looking at it from the outside, that's most interesting. When I went back to do medicine, to do medical research a few years ago, what drove me out of it again was really the spectacle of the megalopolis. It was like Fritz Lang's *Metropolis*: hundreds and hundreds of post-docs trudging to their labs for fear that if they didn't publish they'd be chucked out. They are proletariate. They're exactly as they are in Fritz Lang's *Metropolis*, and I thought, I don't want to be bothered with it at all. I'd much rather be a disreputable gypsy again.

Dr. Patrick:
I would like to pick up on that. As you know, Arnold Roland has called what's happening in medicine the medical industrial complex, which is taking on a life of its own, and I gather this week we are now at the 20th anniversary of the first heart transplant. We really are facing in medicine a very important distinction between high-tech, high-powered medicine and then what might be called low-tech, low-touch kinds of things. Can you comment on that a little bit? Where is that all going to lead us?

Dr. Miller:
I don't know. Again, it is so easy to come out with windy wisdoms of one sort or another. I really don't have any at all, except that something like this is undoubtedly happening. There is this vast medical industrial complex. It's become something where very, very huge endowments work, where there are very high expectations of high technical productivity. People expect there to be transplants and things of that sort, although it doesn't touch the lives of really more than about 10% of the patients. But, nevertheless, it's part of the national prestige, or part of the prestige of the West, and that's what we do. That's what we have to offer to people. I think it is very hard to withhold it once you have discovered it. You can't withhold it. You can't say we're not going to have heart transplants at all because there would be outcries. There would be people having Gregorian calendar riots, people asking for their eleven days back again. You'd have people say, "We must have our transplants. I don't want one, but we must have them available." The bother is, I think, that it's become so expensive. That really is the difficulty. People don't know how to actually fund it. In the long run, they don't know how to fund it. We don't know how to fund it in England, and I don't think you quite know how to fund it here. The National Health Service is falling to bits at the moment. It used to be quite easy in the 1940s or in 1948 when the Labor Party put it together. It was quite clearly a plausible philanthropic scheme, the alternative to which was inconceivable. It wasn't as was seen here—creeping Communism or galloping socialism or any other form of objectionable, un-American activity. It was strictly humanism and philanthropy. But the reason why it was easy

to do in 1948 was that there wasn't much to offer. It didn't cost very much to do it. It was administered at really a comparatively low price. But now when there is such a lot to offer and what is offered is so expensive—it becomes increasingly more expensive—it's terribly hard to finance it as a government institution. The alternative—one that is equally invidious—is trying to actually live off the private sector so that only the rich can afford it, so that you can have rich heart transplants or occasional charitable cases done for the poor where, in fact, a deserving bum is taken off the street and given a heart transplant, rather like that television program "Queen for a Day," so that what you have is a sort of capricious benefit handed out to a poor beggar, like a fairy story. "You will have a heart transplant."

"Oh, thank you!"

We don't know how to put it together.

Dr. Patrick:

Given your understanding of the history of medicine, do you see leadership within medicine capable of dealing with this, or must something come in from outside of the medical establishment or enterprise?

Dr. Miller:

I don't think doctors are very good at that sort of thing because they are so busy doing the daily work of medicine that they are not very good at administering or seeing the thing as a service, and too many doctors in this country are just busy lining their pockets with money. That's what they're in it for. I go around to a lot of campuses and meet a lot of medical students and a lot of young doctors, and I have become increasingly aware of the fact that a lot of young doctors in this country are in it for the condominiums and the powerboats. What they get out of it is big bucks, and it's disgusting, I think, and they're hateful young people. I'd stop them getting hands on patients miles off. I don't know how it ought to be organized really in order to get it better. I think that there's a reaction to it, something which I find equally repulsive, which is this sort of Shirley MacLaineism—the idea that the alternative to high-tech mega-science medicine is getting back to the roots of human primitivism—naturopathy and the whole enchilada, as they say. I find that objectionable as well. The wild lunacies of particularly Californian medicine seem to me to be repulsive. I just think actually that an awful lot of medicine is best conducted at a fairly low-tech level because most people actually are not very seriously ill but need to be looked after and humanely dealt with without having to use gigantic pieces of equipment. But you see doctors themselves don't feel themselves to be prestigious unless they're manipulating these pieces of apparatus. They also feel they are not doing the sort of medicine that their self-sacrificing parents got them into it for. They want to be seen manipulating expensive pieces of apparatus because that's what makes a doctor look good. The number of students who want to go into family medicine, for example, is comparatively small in England. They feel they are not prestigious or charismatic unless they're in the hospital service, particularly in the high-tech science of it. It's not prestigious to be looking after people with Alzheimer's Disease, to be looking after old people or the people who are chronically or spiritually disabled. It's not glamorous. There is blue-chip medicine, and then there's what is sort of third-world medicine, and most medicine is actually third-world medicine. It's just simply dealing with the disabled, the unfortunate, the mildly ill, rather than people with catastrophically interesting and rare diseases. I think this began even when I was a medical student. I remember when I was training in college in London, I knew everything about pheochromocytoma, but I hardly saw an ordinary case of essential hypertension because there were these sort of cavernous diseases that came in for which there were very, very interesting high-tech research programs, and I didn't learn actually what the function of medicine was in the community. Over the last twenty-seven years I have seen my wife do that because she actually is a family doctor, and I can see that's where most medicine is—people running, coming in and out on a daily basis with all sorts of aches, miseries, pains, limps, and sometimes old people who are becoming vague and forgetful and ultimately demented. I just think that that ought to be something which ought to be trained for a great deal more. I'm also obviously advising people to be more rational in their lives in what we call preventive medicine. Preventive medicine is nothing really more than what, in fact, was already encouraged with Hippocratic medicine, which is just simply sobriety and chastity.

From audience:
That's tough to deal with on this campus.

Dr. Miller:
But that then becomes a social issue, you see, and in the end you have to talk about Jerry Falwell types ranting for chastity and sobriety. You have to, as it were, make it look as if it's rational procedure and that there are better ways of living. As Chekhov once said about his plays, "My plays are really inclined to say to people, 'My friends you live badly. Please do not live like that.'" That really is what one wants to do rather than just simply rant about Sodom and Gomorrah, which is what these idiot preachers do. It's a terrible thing, but morally one has become monopolized by the moralistic. That's the aspect which I think ought to be emphasized in medical schools in training, and so forth. I also encourage doctors to spend more time just simply examining patients with their hands because I think you'll get to find out most of the things that are likely to be seriously wrong with people with your hands. You have to use high technical equipment from time to time. But I think people forget when they're doing medicine that the examining of the patient is part of the cure. You tend to think that it is only diagnostic. But actually the extent to which doing that is therapeutic is enormous. It brings you within hands' length with the patient, arms' length of the patient. It's a caress, a precaution. Caresses are not just simply probes, and I think

young students today are inclined to hustle the patient off to the machine in the belief that that's the better result. Obviously, the way of backing up your hunches, your eyes and ears with a machine is good, but I think you get closer to the patient, and in the end that's really what the best sort of medicine is, when you really do have a relationship with the patient. That's not done by any psychiatric seminars on the subject.

Professor Kaplan:
Following that up, we are entering an era now where high-tech medicine is really drama, and it's almost part of the entertainment that we encourage. For example, the news covers every liver transplant that we have. Public institutions are really faced with this problem. Each liver transplant that's reimbursed out of public resources may mean thousands of inoculations for children that we have to forego. How can we make those exchanges between little benefits for lots of people versus big benefits for a few hundred people?

Dr. Miller:
I think it's very hard, this business of how you slice up the cake. It's extremely difficult. I really would hate to offer any advice on the subject. I do think that one's got to be very bold about these things and just simply indicate what the priorities are, in fact, the great community in a sort of Benthamite way, that the greatest happiness to the greatest number really is what should prevail. Now that doesn't mean that someone that is, as it were, liverless should go begging. Every effort should be made to supply them with that. Since liver transplants actually have got a good record, while heart transplants on the whole have not—it's not that bad, but in terms of cost effectiveness it's not that good—I just think that we want liberal funds poured into what, in fact, gives the greatest happiness to the greatest number and, therefore, things like inoculations for children, better health programs, and the more favorable, the humane treatment of the demented elderly, I think is really very, very important. But, you see, all these things are actually not. The thing that maddens me the most about it is there isn't that much shortage of funds anyway. There is only shortage of funds because pigheaded presidents and people actually think that illness is culpable and poverty is culpable, and that actually what you have to do is to blame people for not paying for themselves. There's plenty of money around. If you can spend as much money as we do for all sorts of international enterprises of one sort or another, there is plenty of cash around for dealing with what, in fact, is the most precious commodity in the Commonwealth, which is our shared health. I always feel this, but we don't hold our individual health as a private thing. It's held in trust for everyone else. In the same way John Donne says, "Ask not for whom the bell tolls. It tolleth for thee." In fact, each man's death diminishes me. In the way that each man's death diminishes me also in a very important sense, every man's and woman's health augmenteth me, and we are investing in each other; it is a public commodity. It's a commonwealth, and I do

think that both in England and America—worse in America than in England, although with the monstrous Mrs. Thatcher, we are going the way that you are—there is a diminishing sense of this thing called a commonwealth, that we actually hold things in common, and that these things that are held in common do not diminish our individuality as those who are rabidly fearful of Communism think. They actually enhance our individuality. Our individuality is actually conferred upon us by the degree to which we share certain things. That mustn't, as it were, stop us from doing and enjoying the things which we believe to be our birthright. God forbid that we should live under the sort of system that they do behind the Iron Curtain. I spent a lot of time there, and I know what it's like. Nevertheless, we shouldn't let fear of what goes on there prevent us from humanizing what goes on here, and I think there is such a demented dread of the collectivization of things which do belong to us all that we actually don't take these issues of public health seriously enough. There's plenty of money to do both liver transplants and inoculations. It's really, in the end, mad to think that you have to make the choice between one or the other. They can both be done if only you think that there are other things which are really idiotic to spend money on.

Dr. Patrick:
Often, however, it seems that the definition of the commonwealth that you speak of falls to the media, and they seem not to be doing a very good job with this. This is really an anecdotalization of the process, again, the heart transplant, the liver transplant, the chimpanzee transplant in the chest of the infant. Those are the things which capture the public's fascination.

Dr. Miller:
Well, they do. But then also don't forget that the media are part and parcel of the industrial complex of this country, that they are fastened to advertising. They are themselves part of huge technical corporations which have heavy investments in this particular view of life. As you can probably gather, as you can see the atmosphere of redness spreading from the stage here, I am, in fact, a socialist. I am not a Communist. I'm a socialist. I do believe that these things actually can be done without diminishing individual freedoms when you are committed to the idea that things are being held in common. Television doesn't go along with these ideas, but that's also because it has a commitment to vulgar sensationalism. This thing is a vicious circle, and we encourage that in the public by going on and doing more of it. The public is interested in it.

Dr. Patrick:
You are certainly someone with a foot in both camps, who has worked well within the arts, the media, and has been a powerful force in them. Do you see it possible? Do you see a public-health responsibility on the part of the media?

Dr. Miller:

No, I don't think it's public health, but the media could be much more intelligently used to simply redirect people's interest to things which are less sensational than liver transplants. It isn't just liver transplants. There has to be more sympathy for all sorts of things which happen in the public media now which encourage people to believe what are the good things in life, what is worth looking at, what is worth enjoying, and what is worth having. Just knowing things is nice, and television doesn't actually encourage people to think that. Bertrand Russell said this a long time ago. I seem to hear that cracked old voice of his saying just before he died, "How nice it is to know things!" I believe this to be true, and I think that television actually doesn't really discharge its responsibilities in that area. It has fatuous game shows. It advertises all sorts of idiotic ideas of success, glamour, and it not only depraves the imagination of its audience and turns them into fools in the name of advertising and commerce, but also purports all sorts of ideas of what is prestigious and worth having. We encourage people to think that certain things are worth having, which are actually not worth having at all. I mean like BMWs and that sort. You see, there are a number of kids on a campus like this who are allowed to drive machines like that when they're twenty-two. It's ridiculous that 18-year-old children be given cars of that sort. But you encourage that sort of thing with the television linked to an industrial complex in the way that it is, leading people to think that the liver transplant, in a way, is a symbol of all that.

Professor Kaplan:

With regard to media, people say that the theatre is dying in this country. A friend of mine recently remarked that Broadway in New York is only for tourists now. Yet in Eastern Europe people still turn out for poetry readings. Is that cultural, or is there something that you can tell us about it?

Dr. Miller:

I can tell you a little bit about it because I've seen it in both Eastern Europe and here and England. It's part of this depraving process which I have talked about. Give capitalism its head, really let it ride, and it rides just as roughshod as Communism does over people. The victims enjoy the ride better, that's all, while they're actually being trampled to death while it's happening, and it produces a sort of depraving of the imagination. It's very touching and peculiar, the urgency with which the arts are dealt with in the East. Life is horrible in the East. There is no doubt about it. I would not wish to live in Prague. I would not wish to live in Budapest. Yet I felt more alive in ten days in Prague and Budapest than I had done for the previous ten years in the West. I felt the intensity of a sort of sharpness of existence. The only counterpart I can think of, when I was too young to fully experience it, was the sort of invigorating sense that my parents had, and even as a child I sensed, during the Second World War. The sense that one might die tomorrow produced that intensity, and in the East, because in fact you are under pressure, you're invigilated, watched; you have to learn a second language in order to speak, or a second metaphorical language in order to communicate with one another, which produces an intensity of the imagination which is completely lacking in worlds which are completely free, wherever you can get anything you want as long as you have money.

I had a very interesting experience in the previous year. I had been working very closely with a Polish journalist called Ryszard Kapuscinski, who has written a book which some of you may have read, several books, one of them called the *Emperor*, which is about the fall of Emperor Haile Selassie. It's a marvelous book. He spent time in Addis Ababa at the time of the fall of the government and the arrival of Mengistu. He writes this strange account of the fall, which takes the form of the basic reports from the people who had been in the palace retinue. I had long talks with this man. I wanted to make it into a play, but I can't imagine how I could represent Ethiopia. He said, "Bug off. It's not about Ethiopia. Ethiopia is pretext. The Emperor is about Poland, totalitarianism, and language, and it is about being under pressure." In the middle of this book there is one central and fascinating passage, which is about this business of the learning of a second language. He talks about the oppression in the previous five years, just before the Emperor fell, when people were followed by secret police of Selassie all the time, invigilated. They never knew where they were going to be. Ears everywhere, he said, and because of this pressure of overhearing, being invigilated, being pursued, they learned a second language. They became bilingual, he said, in this country. Bilingual wasn't learning another language other than Ethiopian. They went on speaking this language, but they learned to speak in metaphors, complicated, elaborate circumlocutions through which, in fact, they could say things to one another which were impenetrable to the secret police. In exactly the same way when you are in Poland, when you are in Eastern Germany under the pressure of a Communist regime, there is an intensity of the imagination, precisely because, in fact, you are being invigilated, precisely because things are poor, run down, where every object you get from a shop is precious because you have to queue for it for a long time. I can tell you that one of the touching signs in Budapest was 150 people lining up in a shopping mall. What were they lining up for? They were lining up for Adidas shoes. There is something about that sort of oppression which forces the imagination, and poetry becomes for them, and literature becomes for them a life and a guild. It is not a luxury as it is for us. It isn't something you go into a bookshop and buy because you wanted to read some poetry. They read poetry because it is the second language through which they are communicating against the regime. Literature and art don't matter here. That's the awful thing. They matter; they're matters of life and death in the East. You die without it because you can't live your imaginative life. Here you're at liberty to do it.

This has gone rather far from your question about Broadway. Broadway is bad because Broadway is commercial, and it isn't just tourists. It's not tourists altogether. It's tourists, in some respects, in that people come from the other side of the Hudson

River, but they're local. They're people who come from Long Island and New Jersey. They're local people who are coming from the New York area, and they're depraved audiences. They've been depraved into thinking that only certain things are worth going to, worth laying out $100 for. We are gradually—and although not that gradually—we're fairly rapidly diminishing the sense of the past, particularly in this country. For most of the kids out there on campus, life started last Thursday. Vietnam is almost the First World War for them. The idea that there might have been a rich, complicated culture spoken in other languages centering in Europe is inconceivable to most of them. That is why the theatre dies here, because it is not rooted in and acknowledges the fact that, unfortunately—unfortunately for you, perhaps, but it should be not unfortunate—the center of the Western world is still Europe, and America will die culturally unless it comes to terms with the fact that the great taproot of our humanity, our shared humanity as English speakers, is Europe. It's centered on Roman Christianity and on the great huge oak tree that grew out of that world. If we actually sever that root, there's no hope for this country. It will always be a country of shopping malls and *Cats*. *Cats* is regarded as a peak achievement in the theatre.

Professor Kaplan:
Speaking of East/West relations, we are today starting a major summit between the two so-called super-powers. It's no secret that groups like the Physicians for Social Responsibility and their international counterparts have played a major role over the last few years in focusing upon the absurdity of the nuclear arms race. What particular or peculiar role do physicians play in this thing? Why has this group been successful when others may not have been?

Dr. Miller:
They've certainly not been that successful. They are capable of drawing attention of the community to certain risks associated with nuclear weapons and radiation risks, and so forth. What really makes them successful are catastrophes—Chernobyl. You need a catastrophe every now and then to keep people's dander up. There is nothing like an air crash, nothing like an occasional leak, a Three Mile Island or a Chernobyl. Booster doses are required to keep people on their toes. People become indifferent. I don't think doctors are any better at this. They like to think they are. They meet in judiciously grave and furrowed groups to tell the world about the threats. I don't think they are any more eloquent or more effective than anyone else. They dignify their own deliberations with a great deal of zest, but I don't think anyone listens to them particularly. People are deterred by all sorts of other appetites and all sorts of expediencies I think really in the end.

These East/West things—I don't know what it is that determines at this particular moment the desire to get rid of that particular lot of weapons. It's got nothing whatever to do with philanthropy. It has to do with public relations. It's very convenient for Reagan at the moment, just before his presidency collapses into custard, to see himself as having done that. There are all sorts of complicated things going on inside the Kremlin, which makes it advantageous for Gorbachev to do it. It's actually rather dangerous for them to spend as much money as they do on weapons because their economy is collapsing under the weight of a warfare state. It has nothing to do with the fear of nuclear weapons. It has to do with the fact that the economies of both these countries can't stand what they're doing. We like to think the rhetoric runs these things. It doesn't in the end. I am trying to be quite Marxist about this in the larger sense of the word. I do actually think that the material modes of production really determine ultimately large-scale movements of human affairs and that really, if you look back and you pull the cameras back fifty years from now and we ask, why did these two people get together—this strange, birthmarked dictator from one side meet this mindless dunce on the other, you would have to think, why did they have to come together at this particular moment? You see very clearly that economics is the thing really, that Russia is collapsing.

When I was in Hungary last year, you could see they can't get it together under Communism. They can't get it together because they are spending too much money on making these enormous weapons which they run past the great tomb in Red Square once a year. You can hardly buy meat, and the milk is watered in Poland. Nothing works. You can't get a decent health service here. Your social structures are falling to bits here because, in fact, the pie is being cut up the wrong way in both countries. Now that's what got those two men together, not because of any rhetoric. Various groups like professional groups like to think they are leaning on the government and bringing about effects. I don't think doctors have ever produced an effect on anyone, any more than scientists do. Scientists got together and thought they were going to advise people against the atomic bomb. Poor old Oppenheimer and all those people and Einstein deluded into thinking that they could exert pressure. The only pressure they could exert was coming up with the idea from which the atomic bomb was made, not by them saying, "And by the way, don't use it." People don't listen to that. They are prompted in the end by all sorts of hard expediencies and economic motives.

Professor Kaplan:
Let me follow up with something we started with earlier, and then after this I would like to give people in the audience an opportunity to ask Jonathan some questions as well. Taking a step back to the discussion about poetry, you referred to that as the second language. Is rock-n-roll the second language of the current youth in the United States and England?

Dr. Miller:
No, it's their first language. They haven't got a second language. It's fascinating to talk to some of these young students, the more recent students. I was saying to the gentleman who kindly picked me up at the airport to bring me here today, I was saying that in H. G. Wells' *Time Machine*, you remember there's a wonderful group comes

across this tribe called the Eloy, blond, hedonistic, curiously disengaged creatures, who were interested only in pleasure, so hell-bent—hell-bent's too energetic—so engaged in pleasure that they are indifferent even to the misfortunes that might occasionally befall one of their own number when they're eaten by the Morlocks. Open the door, and there they are. They are right here. I don't know what's happened. It is very, very strange. It started with all those Troy Donahue movies. It's broken out like wildfire again, and I think it's something you get in this culture that you don't get in the East. That's a great pleasure, not to see BMWs and Gidgets. Those are not to be seen there, but the awful thing is they want to be. That's why they are queuing up for Adidas shoes.

Professor Kaplan:
What is the punk movement in England telling us about what's happening?

Dr. Miller:
Well, the punk movement, they're actually finished in England. There aren't any punkers any more. All that's over. There aren't any punks. There are just these people in Benetton clothes, and that sort of bland Benetton world has overtaken everything. Punk is all over after a brief outburst in England. Is there very much of it here now? That sort of heavy metal, hard-drug-taking stuff, is really rather gone from England, and I suspect it's gone from here. There is just the desire to have these Ralph Lauren clothes and BMWs and just consume in a bland generalized way, and party.

From audience:
They may not be punk, but they are majoring in business.

Dr. Miller:
Well, yes, but that's the thing. Punk has given way to Yup instead, you see. I think that that's just awful. It's awful because it denies the idea of our having a previous existence. It denies the notion of culture. By culture I don't mean what books or art galleries you go to, but culture in a deep, anthropological sense of the word. We are four-dimensional creatures who are immersed in our past and who are descendants of ancestors who were committed to another form of life. It seems proper and fitting to know about our antecedents, and a culture which does not know that, I think, is just doomed. There is no point in it carrying on. You might as well pull the plug on the enterprise altogether. I certainly don't want it. I don't want to be amongst it. I am glad I won't be around to see it flourish fully. You must feel this here, surely. I see an older group here. You must feel some kind of despair about it.

From audience:
Wouldn't you say this is one of the things that was done in this age of mass media. We had great respect for our medical tribe. Several of them said, "You guys start

dropping these bombs all over this place, you're all going to die, horribly, and we can't do a bloody thing about it." I think perhaps it really shook people up.

Dr. Miller:
Well, did it? I wonder. I really do wonder about that.

From audience:
Well, for a month it did.

Dr. Miller:
Yes. It has happened that the doctors have deliberated, and you've actually had changes in social policy or social conduct as a result of it. It certainly has happened with smoking, and I find it hard to understand why precisely that has occurred when there are other things it hasn't affected at all. I don't think that doctors deliberating on these things really do have very much effect. I think that every now and then what you do get are fads of fear which very briefly call to conduct. I mean about the lead in petrol, and so forth. Doctors will say something about it, and then it produces pressure groups. I don't think it's doctors really getting together. It is leakages from the profession which produces it rather than doctors explicitly deliberating on that. What happens is there is a leakage. It gets out. The research group discovered that a particular trace element is actually dangerous for you and that it is getting out from some industrial process. It's that that causes protest movements which might eventually result in legislation or in changes of social conduct. It's very rarely doctors getting together deliberately and making statements which cause this. I don't think it's "the Surgeon General has determined that..." which actually stops people as they pick up a cigarette. It's got around; it's leaked progressively that it's pretty risky and it's dangerous, and that changes conduct, I think. I'm being provocative here, but I just think that the professional groups in their narcissism do like to think that they have effects, and I think that they don't on the whole. The things that do produce effects are often quite inadvertent, unexpected, and leakages are much more effective than press releases.

From audience:
You seem so wise that I am going to ask you something that is probably impossible to answer. Do you think that we are actually also sliding down toward some dreadful ending, not just in America but also in Europe—which I see just more and more—as it were, contaminated with this whatever you want to call it? When you look at television here, for example, it's linked to the industrial complex. I thought well, of course, it is. Why haven't I thought about that before and put it in those words to myself? Obviously it is. A disturbing thing is happening in Sweden, which is my home country. Television is just contemplating moving from being noncommercial to switching to commercialization, and I feel that that is a nonreversible process. Once

it happens you are on that slide; you're going, and it's entropy taking over. Is there anything that can be done to stop this development? Could you go to Sweden and talk sense with them?

Dr. Miller:
I'm very upset to hear that Sweden is going the same way as England. England is doing the same thing. England has already got a commercial television channel, but already under the pressure of Mrs. Thatcher, that monstrous and horrible woman, she wants to sell it off. She doesn't understand that it is actually one of the few remaining nobilities of my country. It keeps the thing pure. You know, there's a wonderful essay that was written, a book written by a social administrator and professor of social administration at the London School of Economics, who wrote on the blood transfusion service called *The Gift Relationship*. He talks about the fact that what makes the blood transfusion system in England work and why it's so good is that it's free, that it would not be good if you had to pay for it. It would be less good. It would be much better funded, but precisely because of the source of the fund, it would be less good. It's precisely because people are committed to the notion of it being, again, a shared thing. I think that television is, in fact, like a river. It's a stream which cannot be polluted. Once you allow pollution into it, it's done forever. You kill the organisms in it, and you kill the weeds and the fish and everything. This is precisely what happened. Occasionally in the morning, when I'm sleepless after traveling around the United States, I turn on the television and see things at 6:00 o'clock, 7:00 o'clock, and sometimes later than that when I go to bed. You watch the mindless intrusion of these cajoling and persuasive advertisements which infiltrate like some virus. You see the virus has not just simply infiltrated the interstices between the programs, but it has determined what the programs are, that they're all shit, that you are eating shit all the time, that there is nothing worth seeing. Not only is it not worth seeing, but it exerts a positive, destructive, depraving effect on the imagination of the audiences and particularly the young people. It's mindlessly idiotic; it proffers a view of life which is completely horrible, and this is actually going to happen in countries which do sell themselves. I do believe it will happen in Sweden, and it is happening in Europe. We are committed to the commercial, and it's the end of us. I don't think we're going to slide down towards something terrible. There's going to be no cataclysm. Cataclysms are in a way rather a relief because there's this big Gotterdämmerung. It's not. It's the fact that it's a slow slide to inanition so that looking back fifty years later we will say, "My God, how did we get to be like this?" because the increments are comparatively small, and they are not noticeable as they gradually infiltrate us. I don't know what's going to happen to us in the end. I don't particularly feel pessimistic about it in the sense that I don't actually feel that there's any particular reason to feel optimistic about us as a species really. We are an accident anyway with this sort of funny little fidget in a sleazy, provincial suburb of the cosmos that has actually thrown up this lot. There's no reason to think there is a particular reason for it to be a good outcome. I

think we dignify ourselves by thinking that it's going to end with a huge, big bang. That's very dramatic and exciting, and it's actually rather invigorating to think there's going to be a vast nuclear winter. Carl Sagan gets very excited, and that's all, but it's not going to be like that at all. It's just going to be shopping malls forever, like that wonderful thing that Clifford Geertz, the anthropologist, had when he was talking to a subject in Java. He was trying to get information about their view about the cosmos, and he was talking about how the cosmos was supported. The man said, "Well, it stands on the back of an elephant."

Geertz said, "What does the elephant stand on?"

"On a turtle. The turtle stands on another elephant, and that on a turtle."

He said, "What does the turtle stand on?"

He said, "After that it's turtles all the way down."

Well, I think that actually it's shopping malls all the way down, shopping malls and commercial television and heart transplants and BMWs and Benetton shirts, a sort of depraved, easily subtle hedonism which is not so bad, but not too good either, and certainly nothing we would want to be proud of for being human.

Professor Kaplan:

Following that up, some years ago I did a consulting job for ABC television. What they told me was that what they were doing in television was really the ultimate application of behavioral science because they had studied people's responses, and they had studied the human emotion, and this is what they came up with, and further they argued that they had really tried to put real drama on television. It didn't work very well because the ratings were low and that ultimately what they were doing was really giving people what the human spirit responded to. What do you have to say about that?

Dr. Miller:

They're right. I don't think they're doing behavioral science. They're just doing what, in fact, everyone knew all along. We're seduceable, weak, lazy people as a species, and you can cater to that very easily. You don't have to be a behavioral scientist to know that. That goes back to what I was saying. There is no art in this thing, the idea that you have to somehow have complicated academic disciplines to know what, in fact, the witty and the wise have known from the outset, that we're lazy swine and easily seduced. Of course, that's what we want very easily. What you do is you swim against the current. That's what Jesus Christ was doing. He was swimming across the current. He was saying, "Gentlemen, it's not a good idea to do what you are doing." That's what is so admirable and invigorating about the Bible. I don't happen to be a Christian, but I enjoy reading it because he says things which are really on the whole commendable. He's swimming against the current. He's saying that you're not going to be happy if you actually think you are going to load yourself with goods. You're not going to get into the Kingdom of Heaven if you spend all your money trying to buy BMWs and Benetton shirts and so forth. But he's going against the current. That's behavioral science of a very much more distinguished sort. It's just simply to run against the current—moralism—and as I said, sad that moralism should be in the hands of the moralists and of the utterly, utterly repulsive figures like Haworth and his stripe. Yes, you can easily make it look as if that's what people want. We know what people want very easily. People also want public executions. We could get vast, vast, vast ratings by actually tearing people limb from limb in Rockefeller Plaza. You could have vast crowds turned up to see regicides disemboweled in the 1660s. All through the late Elizabethan period Catholics were torn limb from limb on Tyre Hill to vast crowds and didn't need any social psychologists to tell them that that's what they would like. They didn't go to Elizabeth and say, "Well, we have actually determined that 80% of people interrogated would quite like to see someone have their tongue torn out and they would prefer on balance to see someone with molten lead poured up their rectum." You know these things. You know perfectly well that that's what people would prefer to see, so it's idiotic naivete of television to think that it's doing something according to laws of human psychology. It's doing what everyone knew all along.

Professor Kaplan:
Who currently, though, is swimming against the tide, against upstream?

Dr. Miller:
I don't think there are many people. They are the upholders of culture who do this. This is what, in fact—when Shelley talked about the poets being the unacknowledged legislatures of the world—poets and people who write serious literature in the great tradition do. They are upholding what, in fact, is preferable, and they're saying what they believe to be good and what they believe to be valuable and nourishing and affirmative. I don't think there are any great leaders doing this now. That's one of the things which is so depressing about politics. There are no people who actually will come up and say these things clearly, and when they seem to be doing it, it's actually in the hands of people who are so repulsive—moralists. It's in the hands of the right or in the hands of the idiotic left, never in the hands of the liberal. Lost are the days of great liberalism, and I think it's very sad and dreadful thing. In England we have this completely idiotic left and a mindless and depraved right, and the middle ground is not held by decent, eloquent people anymore. That's what's very sad I think.

From audience:
Yes, I wanted to comment that it's not just the people who have a few years who see what I would call the spiritual or cultural bankruptcy of the U.S. I spent some time in Western Europe studying, and while it has bought into the U.S.-California life style to a great extent, it's still not as evolved on that path as California itself. What I find interesting, and I would like you to comment on is this. In a country that's supposedly

full of individuals—and we loudly scream about the rights of the individual—do you see a kind of parity in the fact that the homogenization of culture or reduction of it to almost two dimensions in fact eliminates that facet of being an individual? I mean, it's all buying BMWs. I'm going after the same thing. How individual is that?

Dr. Miller:
I don't know. What is so interesting about human beings is that they're endlessly surprising one with their unexpectedness and their unpredictability. In the midst of all these things which homogenize and uniformize and totalize, individuals spring up and express themselves and say something is wrong and often are very eloquent and strong about it. I mean this is what happens in totalitarian regimes. You believe the human spirit is broken by these things, and someone always stands up. People did that under the Nazis, and they do it under Communism. I think it's harder to do it under this sort of thing because it's so permissive. As I say, the people who were along for the ride across Lake Constance are liking it, and that's much, much harder to protest against, something which is not a tyranny. It doesn't seem to be one. What it seems to be is aghast; it's lovely being here. You see, what's so interesting is that you see the people in the East queuing up for the Adidas, queuing up for days, coming up to you in the street and asking you whether you want to change dollars so that they can buy denim. Now, what I think happens with that sort of tyranny is that it's very hard to know you are being tyrannized and, therefore, you are actually drowned before you know it. But, even so, you never know. There are always people as in Aldous Huxley's *Brave New World*. There are the people who just simply resisted, and they say this issue is something I don't like what's happening here. I won't breathe the atmosphere. I am sure that for those of you who teach students, there is a bright, clear eye when you are talking and you know, and they are not fidgeting and giggling at the back, with their feet up on the chairs, and who are arrogant, noisy, and dismissive of their teachers, that somewhere you see a respectful, interested face in the back and you don't know where it comes from or why they resisted, what it is or how they stood out against the current.

It's very interesting to watch these kids who come into class, the way they come into class, that arrogant dismissal of their teachers because their teacher hasn't earned as much as they do—the truculent disbelief that they can be flunked; that they're not good enough; the idea that "What do you mean I am not good enough?" It's inconceivable. But nevertheless somewhere there are always these individuals who stand up against that, who actually want to work hard and want to be better and actually think they're not good enough yet so that even when these depravities are subtle and consented to, there are always these individuals who stand up against it. But I do think it's a very dangerous and evasive process that is happening now. In the West it's happened faster, perhaps, in America than anywhere else because a lot of the 20th century got invented in this country anyway, but it's spreading very rapidly to Western Europe. It's quite hard being in Western Europe. I go back and work there.

I direct plays and operas in Europe, and I love being there, but as each year goes by, it's harder and harder to see what's distinctive about Europe anymore. Italy holds out quite well in places. It's really not bad. France doesn't, though. It's all wind-surfing and Club Mediterranean and Benetton. France is becoming awful. I now find that the best croissants in the world are produced here. I suddenly realized when this whole thing was going the way the world was going in Europe about four years ago when I saw a huge refrigerator container truck crossing when I was going to Holland on the ferry from Scandinavia. I saw this vast, articulated refrigerator truck taking frozen pizza made in Norway to Italy. The Euroworld is just not a thing. It isn't completely mappable onto North America, but it's the same disease—Europizza.

From audience:
What do you think theatre can do to swim against the current?

Dr. Miller:
Nothing, unless someone happens to do it; that's all. There's not much. You can't get theatre off the ground. If the current is strong, as it is, you can't get it off the ground. In this country, for example, you can't get a serious theatre going at all. Broadway, it's hopeless. There is no serious theatre in New York. Theatre can't express itself if people don't want the theatre. Television will confirm that more by its social psychology having proved that people don't want it. They will do something to prevent it.

I did *Long Day's Journey into Night* with Jack Lemmon. Now, Jack is an extremely nice man and actually rather a good actor, but he was acted off the stage, in fact, by the three other people whom no one knew. But none of the reviews noticed the people who weren't famous, but they were actually brilliant performers, and it's gauged one with the celebrity world. You can't get anything going in the theatre without a buoyancy tank of some sort, the buoyancy tank meaning this marquee name. It's all locked together. Celebrity, wealth, consumer are all part of the same business. The West, in general, is fascinated by celebrities, absolutely intoxicated by them. I know from *Tristan and Isolde* that I was involved in Los Angeles. It's an entire celebrity event. Actually, I think it is quite a good production, not as good as it's going to be said to be last night by all the people who rhapsodized about it. They rhapsodized about it because they were high on snorting the cocaine of the fame of its participants. I am actually exempting myself from that, but Hockney and Mehta are California names. They're hype, and that's what made the thing work. The people who came there had to believe that they were actually snorting. They were mainlining fame. That's one of the other big, big commodities that the West gets high on. That's what it enjoys—fame, fashion, style, fizz, pizzazz, W Magazine, all the hundreds of magazines you see now around any airport gift and news shop, *People Magazine*. People would be absolutely astonished in the 16th century, 17th century with a magazine called *People Magazine*. You think this is a magazine devoted to humanism, and it's not. It's not about people at all. It's a very, very fascinating shift of the emphasis on the word, and that, I think, is one of the things that is wrong with this. We've gone chronically mad, really. It isn't even madness on a grand scale, or other interesting scales, glumly mad.

Professor Kaplan:
On behalf of the Faculty Research Council, I would like to thank Jonathan Miller for his comments today. I think it was a very lively and stimulating discussion. If I am reading Jonathan's biography correctly, I think he got his M.D. degree at the time that C. P. Snow was delivering his lecture on two cultures at Cambridge where he was distinguishing between literary culture and the scientific culture, and a direct quote is that "there seems to be no place where these two cultures meet." I think we may have an exception today on this campus in the embodiment of one Jonathan Miller. These two cultures are indeed meeting. We will delight in the remainder of the day, and I would encourage all of you to come to the 4:00 lecture.

President Day:
I'm delighted to welcome you to San Diego State University's Fifth Distinguished Graduate Research Lecture. The Distinguished Graduate Research Lecture series is sponsored by the Graduate Division and Research and the University Research Council, and it's an example of the University's commitment to enhancing the relationship between good teaching and scholarship. The Distinguished Graduate Research Lecture series was developed for the purpose of bringing eminent scientists and scholars of national and international stature to our campus to present university-wide lectures and colloquia on generic problems of research and scholarly activities and graduate education. These have included a combination of public lectures of general interest and smaller seminars or workshops for advanced graduate students and faculty actively pursuing research in related areas. Each academic discipline or department offering graduate degrees has an opportunity to nominate and sponsor the notable scholars who are invited to present the lectures. The faculty committee of the University Research Council, with representatives from each of the seven colleges, makes recommendations to the graduate dean regarding the final selection.

Previous Distinguished Graduate Research Lecturers have included the distinguished linguist Noam Chomsky of the Massachusetts Institute of Technology; Dr. Arthur Kornberg, professor of biochemistry at Stanford University and Nobel Prize winner in medicine; Professor Nathan Glazer of Harvard University, a renowned scholar on ethnic issues and concerns; and Dr. Jane Goodall, internationally acclaimed ecologist and primatologist. Exposure to and interaction with such distinguished researchers and scholars provides an unusual educational opportunity for the entire university community and has become one of the unique aspects of the graduate school experience at San Diego State University. I know that our Fifth Distinguished Graduate Research Lecture, presented today by Dr. Jonathan Miller, will be a most significant highlight in this important tradition of academic enrichment.

I would now like to present Dr. James Cobble, Dean of the Graduate Division and Research, who will introduce our honored speaker. Thank you.

Dean Cobble:
Jonathan Wolf Miller was born on July 21, 1934, in London, the son of Emanuel Miller, a distinguished child psychiatrist, and biographer Betty Miller. Educated during the turbulent days of World War II in England, he studied at St. John's College at Cambridge in natural science and qualified as a doctor of medicine at University College in 1959.

It was at Cambridge while reading history and the philosophy of science that he first was persuaded to perform in the university's Footlights Theatricals. After graduation while immersing himself in his chosen medical specialty, neuropathology, and on the way to a career in research and teaching, he supplemented his intern's salary by appearing in late-night stints in various London cabarets. It was during a two-week break between terms at University College Hospital in 1959 that it was proposed that he both co-write and co-star in a review, *Beyond the Fringe*, at an Edinburgh arts festival. It has been said that as far as his medical career was concerned *Fringe* was a disaster, but it would come to be hailed by critics as marking a revolutionary change in the comedy of the theatre. We do not know why Physician Miller tempted the fates by thinking that a short excursion into the theatre for just about a year would be both fun and profitable and after which he could return to the serious business of medical academics. Some year! That was twenty-eight years ago. The Fringe took him to New York where he also contributed to the *New York Review of Books* and the *Partisan Review*. In 1965, he returned to London to begin a distinguished career in television with the BBC, producing the series on the history of medicine, *The Body in Question*. From then on, attempting to chronicle his career is like attempting to describe a type of intellectual and artistic tornado.

During the following years he was to become a renowned playwright and a theatre, TV, and opera director. He adapted new strategies to the staging of old classics at a time when such experimentation was not easy and was received with some hostility. For example, his London production of Verdi's *Rigoletto* was staged as in a Mafia-ridden Brooklyn of 1950, and his rendering of *Much Ado About Nothing* was placed in the time during World War I. One BBC executive, whose criticism will probably be remembered longer than his intellect, on hearing that Director Miller had agreed to produce twelve Shakespearean plays for British television, was said to have moaned, "I hope he's not going to do them underwater."

In 1983, after twenty-five fruitful years as a veritable one-man festival of the arts, Artist Miller vowed to leave the theatre. The words "battle fatigue" and "never again" were heard, and he did do a two-year fellowship in neuropsychology at the University of Sussex. History notes, however, that after that two-year academic excursion, he returned to the stage actively directing opera while keeping alive his more recent interests in brain research, memory, and imagery.

As an author, director, producer, scientist, investigator, and teacher, Dr. Miller has made a success of many careers and has been able to create innovative relationships between the sciences and the arts. His stage writings are full of mathematical and scientific analogues, and he has written books on medical history and the nature of psychology and the language of thought.

He has been honored in many ways. I mention but a few: an Honorary Fellow of St. John's College at Cambridge; honorary doctorates of literature, both universities of Leicester and Kent; Commander of the Order of the British Empire, received from Queen Elizabeth II; the Silver Medal of the Royal Television Society; and numerous invited lectures at many universities. His artistry and humor have helped make our world a better place in which to work and live, and his role as an intellectual provocateur is at the cornerstone of intellectual inquiry, research, and creativity and one which the universities hold dear to their hearts and strive to nourish. Today, we, too, honor him for these contributions. Mr. President, members of faculty, students and staff, and friends of the university, it is my great pleasure to present the Distinguished Graduate Research Lecturer for 1987, Jonathan Miller.

Dr. Miller:

I must confess, Mr. President, that when I heard the list of the previous lecturers, which I heard for the first time just three minutes ago, I felt like Danny Kaye in one of those movies where he blundered onto the stage, in the wrong place, not knowing the script, and made the wrong appointment. I feel this for several reasons connected with the rather disreputable career which you have just heard outlined. I'm a fugitive from a respectable profession, from medicine, and I did, in fact, make this unrealistic decision believing that I could return from the theatre after a year, return to medicine and pursue the interests that I had always had as a child in the functioning of the brain. Indeed, twenty-eight years later I find myself still in this disreputable profession which I think of somehow as being inappropriate for a member of a series of lecturers which include the people you mentioned. The reason why I feel this is, I think, somehow part of the cultural view that we all have of the theatre, and it reflects something which I suppose has a bearing on my attitude to the work that I do in the theatre now.

It's extremely hard to convince many people, either in the universities or, indeed, in the community at large, that there is anything important or serious about the theatre. Lip service is paid to it, and I've often thought of the irregular verb "theatre-goer," which is defined as follows: I go to the theatre; you are interested in drama; *he* is in show biz. It is a feeling, which I've often felt in my years in the theatre, that there is something curiously disreputable about it as practiced. It's disreputable to be in it; it's disreputable to be a protagonist; it's disreputable to be a director; and, above all, an actor or an actress. It's quite respectable to study it; it's quite respectable to write theses about the history of the theatre but very disreputable to be a performer in it.

I've often found myself asking, "Why is it? What is there peculiar about this profession which actually renders it off to the edge of serious human enterprises?" so that science and the arts and literature are regarded as permanent contributions to what is important to human affairs, but somehow what we do on a raised stage, illuminated, is not. I think there are lots of reasons for this. One, I think, is naturally a thing which goes back perhaps to Plato, which is a suspicion of representation, a suspicion of something which is a lie, a pretense. There is a very peculiar pejorative term which was used by the Victorians to describe a deceptive woman, a woman who, in fact, was liable to deceive her husband. She was described often as a consummate actress. How odd that something which was, as it were, the peak, the paradigm of an achievement, should be regarded as a nadir of morality! But to be a consummate actress was to be disreputable in some way. To be a consummate performer in this particular field is, in fact, regarded as disreputable, and I think that there is a natural suspicion of this particular art form that has to do with pretense; it's to do with "putting on airs;" it's to do with putting on makeup; it's to do with putting on masks, of not being someone who, in fact, is yourself but being someone else. Then, above all, there is this peculiar aphrodisiac atmosphere that hangs over the theatre, that which goes on backstage is what we all sneakily like to indulge in but only actors, actresses, and above all, directors have a chance to get their hands on. The casting couch looms large in the fantasies of those who despise the theatre; but there is this thought that the theatre is, in some strange way, disreputable, tawdry, picaresque. I think it is in some way connected with its role as representation. For some reason this doesn't attach itself to pictorial representation. It's something about people using their physiques, their bodies, in order to represent something. It's people using themselves to be some other self which lies behind this suspicion of the theatre.

But there is also much more, I suspect. There is a fundamental reason that really has a bearing on what I want to talk about this evening. That is, that its achievements, unlike any of the other arts that are respected, are so much more ephemeral. While, in fact, you can write for theatre and the work remains and the work survives, the work remains to be discussed and analyzed and celebrated in the groves of academe, the work of the performer and the work of the producer or director, who is a comparative newcomer to the theatre, does not survive. It is, in fact, essentially ephemeral; and we dread and suspect the ephemeral. We tend to think that anything which can be that ephemeral must in some strange way, and by that very token, be valueless.

If you put these two factors together—the factor of our suspicion of the use of the human body, the use of the human self to represent other selves, selves other than the one that you are, with this quality of the ephemeral, the transient, and so forth—I think you can understand why it is that this form of art, which I very strongly maintain to be an art on a par with all the other, on a par with the beaux-arts (it is one of the beaux-arts), stands aside. Why it is set aside; why it is regarded as something trivial; why it is that when I confronted my aging father—a distinguished, significant, and important psychiatrist in a distinguished, important, and significant field (when I was 40 I would visit him in his flat, his apartment)—he would still, confronted by a son of 40, say to him, "Well, have you decided what you're going to do?" I think that again it came from this suspicion of something which was using the self for purposes other than the proper use of the self, and also it was ephemeral. There was nothing, he felt, and I often feel it myself, there was nothing to show for it. It could be put on tape, perhaps, but ultimately there was nothing to show for it. The art work which, in fact, remains when Chekhov puts pen to paper, the art work which survives when Chardin puts paint brush to canvas . . . there is no counterpart to that in the work which we do, either as performers or directors. At the last performance it will remain in the memories of those who witnessed it. That will be handed down by story, by anecdote to people, and people will hear, "Oh, you ought to have seen his *Three Sisters*, or his so-and-so." But finally, there is no record. There is only the witness, and there is only the cold, browning notices in the newspapers. This is one of the things that drives producers and actors mad in the end and why we get battle fatigue perhaps moreso than painters and writers. We cannot hold an object out ten years later and say, "This is still here. We still have this. We can refute the critics." There is no refutation of the critics.

I remember seeing in the Jeu de Paume in Paris the noble, arrogant, aphrodisiac figure of Manet's *Olympia* staring defiantly down the perspectives of posterity at the critics whom she could now defy on behalf of Manet. Rejected, despised by the critics who are Manet's contemporaries, he or she is arrogantly naked on her bed saying, "Screw you. Manet was better than any of you." We in the theatre have no such naked figure on the couch who can, in fact, present herself to the critics of yesteryear and confront posterity and say, "This was the achievement."

For that reason there is this peculiar suspicion that surrounds the theatre so that, therefore, when I talk about the afterlife of plays, I'm talking also about the afterlife of productions. I suppose in an autobiographical and melancholy sense, I am talking about my own autobiography. I am talking about the autobiography of all of us who worked in the theatre, whose work will die with us, and who spend our lives working on and elucidating and developing artists who have the pleasure and the privilege of knowing that their works will outlast any particular production of their works. In other words, we work on Shakespeare, on Wagner as I did yesterday evening, on Chekhov and innumerable people who, in fact, will be remembered long after our handiwork has been forgotten. In a way I want to commemorate work which is incommemorable, which does not survive, and I want to talk about some of the problems that go with working in the theatre and talk about the art work that directors perform.

The reason why I have chosen the term "The Afterlife of Plays" is to show you what directors do, and what the fate of a text is, and why it must necessarily undergo change with the passage of time, and that this change is best inflicted upon the work deliberately rather than, as it were, by default, which tended to happen before the director appeared on the scene. In recent years, and as you can judge from that brief quotation of some of the criticism that was leveled at me, there has been an almost consistent chorus of disapproval of the work of the director so that the director really has much more reason for neurosis than even the performer. In the last twenty years, though perhaps it is diminishing in intensity now, there has been a consensus, both on the part of audiences and on the part of critics, that we are a wicked lot. We are, in fact, Mongol hordes who ride roughshod over great texts, great scores, and great scripts, and use them to do things which were not intended by their authors or by their composers. Others feel these works are best left to speak for themselves, to be done as they were originally done, to present the canonical version which will deliver the meanings and ideas of the author or composer involved. Now my point is that I believe that change, transformation, mutation in any way is, in fact, the nature of these works. Any work which depends for its survival on continuous and intermittent reproduction is going to undergo transformation and change whether you like it or not. It is much better that the changes are at least the result of art work rather than the result of curious, careless negligence, and worst of all when they are the changes inflicted by those who believe that they are actually bringing about uniformity and no change whatsoever.

In a way, I think this is very comparable to the mutations and changes which are the result of sexual reproduction in living organisms. It is in the nature of these works that by virtue of the fact that they have to be reproduced in order to survive they actually undergo change with each successive reproduction. But I think it is also the case even with works that do not depend on reproduction for survival. Even though a paradigm case of survival without reproduction, in other words paintings and sculptures, there is mutation built into the business whether you like it or not, and people often overlook that.

Briefly I would like to survey the extent to which nonreproductive or autographic works undergo change, as well as allographic works that depend for their survival on reproduction. Paintings and sculptures also undergo change merely by outlasting their makers. The most obvious way in which they do this is by undergoing physical change which is the result of wind and weather. I suppose the most vivid examples are the mutilated statues of antiquity. We all know the torso of Belvedere, the Venus de Milo, and innumerable statues which have only come down to us in fragmented form. Mutilation, physical mutilation, is one of the ways in which these things undergo transformation, simply by lasting. They do not have to be reproduced to change; they change simply by lasting and being damaged.

They also undergo change by being translated to places that were unexpected or unforeseen by their makers. Just think of the paintings that have been moved from churches and chapels where they were, as it were, devices to assist piety and placed on the white walls of galleries where they have been reclassified as aesthetic objects. Something that is hanging on the walls of the Norton Simon Museum or the Getty Museum is simply a different object by virtue of having been wrenched out of the context for which it was originally intended. It is no longer seen in the same way. It may not have undergone a physical transformation in the way that these mutilated statues have, but it has undergone a cognitive transformation in that to see it in such a context is to see it in a totally different way. It's not just that you're not in a religious mood when you go into the Norton Simon or into the Getty, but, by not being in a religious mood when you see it, you see different things in it. It undergoes a distinct, cognitive change just as profound as the change which it can undergo by material deterioration as a result of wind and rain. It's reclassified.

There are other, more subtle ways in which a work becomes reclassified, even within the gallery context, perhaps subtler than the transformation that it undergoes by going from church to gallery. Just think of the way in which a work undergoes cognitive transformation by being juxtaposed in different ways on the walls of the gallery with other works. It reclassifies the work, and it undergoes cognitive change as a result of that. Think, for example, of exhibiting the work of Chardin, whom I mentioned before in an exhibition of Chardin. If you have, as was held in the Grand Palais five years ago, a massive collective exhibition of all Chardin's works, where practically all of them were there—120 or 125 works of Chardin—and you see them, suddenly what is visible in Chardin is totally changed as the result of seeing something which Chardin himself nor his contemporaries ever saw, which is all of Chardin's work placed in consecutive sequence around the walls of a gallery. What is common to Chardin becomes apparent, which has not become apparent when you see Chardin in other contexts. Exhibit a still life by Chardin in a gallery which is devoted to the French 18th century, and you will see things in Chardin which are made salient by virtue of the fact that you are now detecting features common to all pictures painted in France of the 18th century, things which might have remained invisible if it was set in the context of all Chardin's works. There are subtle, cognitive changes that the work undergoes that could not have been foreseen by Chardin when he painted those pictures. First of all, the work is taken out of one context and put into the context of a gallery. Changes are most profound, of course, when it goes from church to gallery, but even when it goes from a domestic interior for which it was intended by Chardin to a gallery, it undergoes a transformation by being juxtapositioned. Here in the world of autographic works, things which, in fact, do not depend for their survival on reproduction, there is change built into the passage of time. By enduring the passage of time, these things undergo cognitive transformation.

I believe, also, that works which have to be reproduced in order to survive are likely to have variation built into them of a much more radical sort, because at least physically there are recognizable connections with the original work since it is material that has survived. If something really doesn't exist at all in between performances, then the possibilities of variations which are built into reproduction are enormous. In fact, there are those who would say that the existence of a play or an opera between performances is logically very ambiguous. To what extent would you say, for example, that *Tristan and Isolde* existed between the rare, successive performances of it? Now it has been said that Shakespeare's plays exist in a very plenary and vigorous form without, in fact, any performances of them having occurred at all. But had Shakespeare's plays been confined to the library shelf from the day they were written to the day we now pick them up, they would still have had a powerful aesthetic existence. There is something extremely forlorn, as one philosopher has said, perhaps even unintelligible, about the idea of unperformed opera. To what extent is it in existence at all? Shakespeare's plays quite clearly are in existence when they are opened as books and read. With the exception of the highly literate musician who can read the score and open it and actually hear sounds when he or she does so, it's extremely ambiguous to the extent to which the work could be said to be delivering itself as a work unless it is performed. We have the work, in a sense, not existing unless performed.

Now let me amplify this a little with regard to plays. There are those who say that certain plays should not be performed—and I leave operas on one side because I think they are a very special case because, as I say, their forlornness is very peculiar when not performed. Let's think about Shakespeare where here there is a case to be made for his plays never being performed. There are those like Charles Lamb who would say that Shakespeare's plays or plays of that magnitude are only reduced or diminished in performance, that they are at their highest and they are at their peak when read by readers with a well-stocked, well-furnished imagination, and that there is a deterioration, an inevitable deterioration, when they are performed. The reproduction is a disaster. Far from being the thing which guarantees their continuity and their survival, it's the thing which actually threatens their survival and threatens their identity. There are those who would say that Shakespeare is best left unperformed.

Now, people who actually underwrite and sponsor this idea of the non-performance of Shakespeare and the idea that their identity is to be seen in the text rather than in their stage performance naturally do allow that Shakespeare allowed performance himself and that, therefore, there must have been something in his mind which saw it as a preferred state for his works. But they would then say they would allow certain minimal versions of performance to fend off some of the more violently deteriorating influences of the performing artists. Now, I suppose the strongest, the most eloquent emblem of this attitude is contained in the belief that the performance done by schoolchildren of Shakespeare is best, that it's purest, the one least inflected by professional attitudes, and the one least polluted by "show biz" vulgarities. In fact, there are many people, mostly to be found in the academic community, who insist that the strongest, the best versions that they have ever seen of *A Midsmummer Night's Dream* or *As You Like It* have been the ones performed by young schoolchildren. They heard Shakespeare clearly. These piping, innocent voices—albeit unskilled, perhaps charmingly naive, often inflecting the verses and words in the wrong way—nevertheless, gave a pure, clear channel to the Bard himself, because there was no complicated, active interpretation imposed by a professional or by people with awful ideas of their own.

I believe this to be nonsense. There is undoubtedly something very charming about schoolchildren's performances of Shakespeare, but I think that what we find intriguing about them has nothing whatever to do with the fact that they are uninflected, clear versions, a hi-fi version of Shakespeare's imagination, but simply because there is a dada shock about the spectacle of seeing such volcanic emotions expressed by such diminutive performers. It's something comparable, I think, to the experience of seeing those little museum showcases which we have occasionally seen in country towns in England of stuffed woodland animals dressed up in frock coats enacting the tennis court oath. It's the discrepancy which we find charming and often that, as it were, jars the imagination and makes us listen to the words more clearly than we might if it was spoken by an adult. But the next level of minimalism that is allowed by people who would prefer to see Shakespeare confined to the library and excluded from the theatre is the idea that it is best performed by amateurs because the amateur himself or herself has not yet come under the influence of the profession, untarnished by the tawdriness of the profession and, above all, untarnished by the intervention of the professional producer or director.

Then, again, that is really always nonsense because most of the performances that you see done by amateurs are good only when the company of amateurs is fortunate to have someone who is good enough to be a professional amongst them. It's not that you're hearing Shakespeare clear; it's that you're seeing, fortunately, if you're lucky that night, a good performance which is being done by people who are good enough to be professionals.

The third level of minimalism is the one that allows it to be by professional actors, regretting meanwhile that they're there, but that exempts the performance from the influence and depredations of a professional producer or director. These things were growing up in England in the sixties and seventies, things called "actors' companies," companies of men, actors who got together and agreed to perform Shakespeare's plays or, indeed, any plays without the intervention of a director. "We can do it all right ourselves," they said, "and we will actually bring these performances to life; we will actually guarantee the fidelity of the performance, because" (in some way and they will argue) "we as performers are in touch with the Bard, because Shakespeare himself was an actor and, therefore, we, in a sense, are green-room cronies of the old fellow, and we know best what he did." These will be undirected works that will not contain a sort of univocal interpretation from one source. But, of course, it's nonsense. It's an ideal which is nonsense for two reasons. One reason is that within about three or four days one of the actors' company by default simply becomes the director. It's often the one with the loudest mouth or the noisiest or the most brutal or the most highly paid or the most famous. Whatever it is, there is always one person three or four days after the rehearsals begin who has taken charge of it and who is imposing upon it his or her view of what Shakespeare means. What I'm saying is that when works which would depend on reproduction depend on successively being performed, it is necessary to have someone who decides how the thing is going to be done and, as it were, who becomes a comprehensive president or chairman of the committee who's going to decide what interpretation is going to be put upon the work, what it is going to mean, what it might have meant to the author, and what it is going to mean for the audience. These are two different things which don't necessarily coincide, nor ought they to coincide. But the intervention of someone who is deliberately appointed to impose interpretation introduces for the first time the idea of control upon what is necessarily a mutational process.

You see, he's a very recent figure on the Western stage, the producer or director, not more than a hundred years old and, probably in his present form, not much more than about thirty or forty years old. Until a hundred years ago plays got on, plays were reproduced, successively reproduced according to the rules of precedent, and stage managers took care of it—actor/managers—and actors themselves took care of it. The plays simply got on, but they got on in the belief on the part of those who were doing them that that's the way it always was done, and they were, in fact, preserved more as identical performances from one generation to the next. Yet when you actually survey specimens, illustrations from the 16th, 17th, 18th, and 19th centuries of what were supposed to be canonical versions of Shakespeare, they look so startlingly different from one another that on certain occasions it's quite hard to know they are illustrations of the same play. You realize they are the same play only because some of the scenes are quite clearly recognizable, and you can actually say it's Hamlet. Very often the illustrations show Hamlet in his mother's closet seeing his father's ghost. Because you can pause the picture, you can infer that this must be *Hamlet* that you're looking at, but actually they're startlingly different, even though each one of those particular performances was done in the belief that no difference was being introduced. They were mutating by default by the mere act of reproduction, by the mere act of putting it on stage at all. The next time it was mutating you have no reason to know unless you are professionally or even amateurishly associated with the theatre, but I can tell you that works mutate from performance to performance within the run of any particular production. If I were to go back tomorrow night or Wednesday night to Los Angeles to see my production of *Tristan and Isolde* which opened last night, I know that there would be quite recognizable changes, changes that even a comparatively uninformed member of the audience would be able to detect. There would be differences in quality. One of the singer's voices might have gone off in the time. One of the singer's voices might have improved. There are all sorts of differences which are simply introduced into the thing by virtue of the fact that it's not the same performance. By doing it again, it cannot be copied. Even when you ask someone to copy, they cannot copy identically. Mozart, for example, as a child, when asked to copy one of his own piano sonatas on the piano, introduced variations. He was rebuked and disciplined, and when they said to do it exactly as he had written it, he couldn't do it. The process of transcription, the process of copying, the process of reproduction, of re-production, introduces novelty. It introduces mutation. It cannot be controlled because that is in the nature of the act of impersonation, the act of forgery, and the act of copying. Acts of copying, forgery, and reproduction involve all sorts of complicated negotiations with the object to be copied.

One of the arguments which I very commonly use when I am talking about this subject in discussing the nature of copying, which is what reproduction is a part of, is a subset of the task of copying, is the forger's art. Now, let's say that we even had at our disposal a visual stereotype, a prototype which would allow us to copy the supposedly canonical version of Shakespeare's first night of *Hamlet*, that supposedly was the one he approved. Would we actually even have a *de facto* chance of copying it without mutation? Well, of course, we wouldn't, and the reason why we wouldn't is shown most clearly by the stories and anecdotes which are associated with forgery. With forgery the name of the game is deception. The game is actually making it identical, identical to the point that it deceives the audience into thinking that they are seeing the presence of the original. Even when you have that as your avowed purpose, and that's not even the avowed purpose of the theatre, the chance of mutation creeps in. Think of the famous story of the van Meegeren forgeries of Vermeer, and it becomes very apparent.

At the risk of boring those who know, I will tell those who don't know, just briefly, what happened with the van Meegeren forgeries of Vermeer. Van Meegeren was a disgruntled artist, a minor artist of really no importance at all, in the thirties in Holland, who felt that he had been rejected by the community of critics and decided to have his own back on them by deceiving them with and passing off his versions of some as-yet undiscovered paintings by Vermeer, which he succeeded in doing. He deceived the famous Dr. Bredius of the Mauritshus who had actually received these and acknowledged that they would now have to enlarge the *oeuvre* of the master to include these works. He passed them off on the market. So far so good. It looks as if the act of copying has worked. This was a rather peculiar sort of copying because he wasn't copying from a prototype. He was copying by analogy with a prototype because he actually was creating a new work, not copying one which was known and then thought to be lost. We now go to the Second World War. Some of these works have entered Nazi hands during the occupation. At the liberation van Meegeren, of course, is now indicted by the Dutch authorities for having collaborated with the Nazis by having sold them to the Nazis. He said, "They weren't Vermeers at all that I was selling. These are not national Dutch art treasures that I was passing off. They were van Meegerens. I painted them."

"Nonsense," they said. "No one could have painted them. Those are Vermeers. It's quite clear to anyone. Look, look; you can see they're Vermeers."

He said, "No, no. They are van Meegerens, and I'll do another one to show you." Indeed, he was forced to paint for the judges other van Meegeren Vermeers.

Now the third stage of the story: thirty years later, forty years later, we now look at the van Meegeren Vermeers, and we look at the real, authenticated Vermeers which providence has guaranteed that we know to be Vermeers, and we look at the van Meegerens which deceived Dr. Bredius in 1938. We now cannot see how Dr. Bredius could have been such a fool. Now there are certain obvious reasons why the two become distinctive when you have two separate classes, as has been pointed out by

Nelson Goodman. But there are much more profound reasons than that. We actually find it hard to think how anyone could have been taken in by these. They are quite clearly different. How could it be? How could it be that something could have deceived high art historical experts in 1938, where even a layman could tell the difference now? It's not that we've got that much smarter. It's not that our historical knowledge has improved by that much, and certainly for the layman who has not been studying art history. That can't be the reason at all, so why is it? Well, I think the reason is perfectly simple, really, simple and complex and has a deep bearing upon our notion of mutation in the theatre and on the role of the afterlife of plays. That is, that what you see in Vermeer in 1938, what you cherish, and what you think is worth forging, what is worth bringing out if you're going to forge Vermeer, is completely different to what you think is worth forging and bringing out in Vermeer in 1987. We cherish Vermeer for reasons that are very different from the reasons that they cherished Vermeer and thought it was worth forging him in 1938. It has a bearing on what I was saying earlier about what happens to pictures when you place them in different contexts. When you put them in different contexts, they cognitively undergo change because you reclassify them. Although, in fact, the physical object hasn't changed, the cognitive object has changed because you have reclassified it, putting it in a different context. You have, thereby, redirected the vision of the spectator that is, therefore, going to guarantee that he or she will see in it different types of salience from the ones that they saw when it was exhibited in other contexts. Well, exhibiting things in different gallery contexts is the same business as exhibiting them in different historical, chronological contexts. To exhibit Vermeer in 1938 is to make it into a different cognitive object from exhibiting it to an audience in the 1980s.

If that happens in the case of forgery where identity is the name of the game, where you actually intend to rule out mutation, where mutation is fatal to your craft, think how much more readily it's likely to creep in when mutation is not even really the name of the game except among the people who are so deludedly foolish into thinking that they actually have a task of making things work in the theatre by reproducing canonical versions. Even if we had got, even if we were lucky—or perhaps it's not lucky at all, and let's consider that in a moment—enough to have a videotape recording, a perfect sound and a perfect videotape recording of the first night of *Tristan* or the first night of *Hamlet*, mutation would creep into the works anyway so that as we copied them they would undergo precisely the same transformation that van Meegeren's forgeries of Vermeer did. What were thought to be perfect copies of the original this year would be looked back on by audiences thirty years later who would say, "How did anyone ever think that they were actually reproducing Shakespeare's work?" I've seen this happen with videotapes of much more recent productions than the first night of *Twelfth Night*, particularly in German opera houses where they offered this, and also where they have a repertoire system which involves having to revive operas many, many years after their inaugural production in order, as it were, to defray the original costs of production. They keep videotapes of all the productions, often shot from a single camera rather like this, and they use those in order to revive the work perhaps five or even ten years later. I've seen what happens when assistant producers go down into the basement and get these things out of the racks and start running them. They get back on the stage and say, "What he did was this. No, no, you come down stage left here," and they go back and look at it, and it never looks like the original. Certainly by the witness of those who saw the original, something has undergone curious transformation. It's mutating already. It mutates less when that tape is being looked at by people who, as it were, can introduce *Verstehen*, *understand*ing, interpretative understanding. In other words, people who were there at the time when the work was first done can see what was trying to be done. But if they don't know what was trying to be done, they can't see what was done, so that when that tape is being looked at by people unconnected with the original production, by assistants perhaps ten years later who didn't even know, who probably weren't even old enough to be present at the inaugural production, they look at that work as if it were an obscure, Egyptian palimpsest. It's hard to read. It's not hard to read because the tape is deteriorated. It's hard to read because you don't know what the intention was. If you are not privy to the intention, you actually don't know what was achieved; therefore, when you start to copy it, you copy wrong.

We are in this very curious sort of time slip when it comes to the reproductive arts, when it comes to plays, when it comes to operas, and when it comes to the performance of symphonies, for that matter. This is why the notion of authentic performances in music is really, in the end, barking up the wrong tree, although it has less variability built into it than the stage. What I want to leave you with before I hope I can start asking for questions from you, is a plea for the artistry that we as producers and performers bring into the field of the fine arts. It isn't something which survives. It is something which decays and also which depends on successive reproduction for its existence, where mutation and change are built into it whether you like it or not. Those of us who are often accused of ravaging these works are, I believe, by our ravages, guaranteeing their immortality.

Now I said that I would return to this question of what would happen if we had the tapes of Shakespeare. We haven't got them, but we do have some interesting analogous experiences which tell us of some of the disasters which can befall works where the prototype or something like the prototype does exist. In those few works where living associates of the inaugural production live on beyond the life of the composer or the author who act as presidents of a custodial committee, we do see very interesting examples of what happens to works when we do have an opportunity to slavishly, or apparently slavishly, reproduce the original, as in the case of Wagner, with the widow Wagner, in the case of Gilbert and Sullivan, and also in the case of Chekhov, with the widow Chekhov. The widows often play a powerful role in this. We have an opportunity to see what would have happened to works if a custodial committee had taken charge of it and guaranteed what they believed to be its immutability. I don't know how many of you ever saw the Moscow Art Theatre productions of Chekhov which came to the West in the 1950s, but those who did bear witness to the fact that they were curiously mummified. Whether or not they were, in fact, transcriptions of the original is debatable because we haven't got the prototype to see. Those in the company thought they were, and they may have been deluding themselves because memory itself is undergoing updating all the time. Nevertheless, to an audience who was unacquainted either with the prototype or with other versions, they looked curiously mummified. There was something odd and stilted about them. How could anyone have liked Chekhov if that was what he looked like in the original? I believe that the same thing happened, certainly, with Gilbert and Sullivan. I had recent experiences of it with the works of Benjamin Britten, where the widow Britten wrote a seven-page blasting attack on the production that I did of *The Turn of the Screw*. She had assumed custodial authority of what would count as a canonical version of the master's original work. In the works that survived that were the products of such custodial committees, you do get this withered appearance.

Perhaps the most vivid example of this was my recent brush with the O'Neill custodial committee. For years, O'Neill has had a custodial committee around him, obviously originally headed by the widow O'Neill, but there were trustees of the widow who continued to maintain the work, and there were the supporters of the work. The work was performed in a reverent way in which length of performance was part of the guarantee of its greatness. *A Long Day's Journey into Night* was, indeed, for the audience as well, a long day's journey into the night. That was an important part of its reputation, and, therefore, the pace of the work guaranteed this length. It was performed very carefully at length. One character finished reciting, and then another character began to recite, and the work lasted over four hours. I came up against this custodial committee when I decided to do it in ways which I felt would bring it to life, by abbreviating the play, not by cutting it, but by getting them to talk normally, by not assuming that it was the Agamemnon, by not assuming that it was an incantation, and by simply making it into a drunken, Irish, Neal Simon comedy in a way. It was fascinating to find that one came up against the custodial committee's versions. When you look at the one living example, surviving example, of the custodial committee's version of the film with Ralph Richardson, you see again how stilted and mummified it has become and how much of an ill service it renders to the author. If Shakespeare himself had had the misfortune to have a custodial committee still alive today, guaranteeing the canonical uniformity of his performances, I suspect that he would have gone back to the library in the form those who prefer to see him would like. These works are at liberty, and they must at liberty undergo the wildest possible reaches of depredation. It is actually going through the risks of ravaging and depredation that the immortality is guaranteed. We who are thought to be the destroyers of these works are in some odd and paradoxical way really the sponsors of their immortality. Thank you very much, indeed.

Dean Cobble:
Thank you very much. We will now have an opportunity for the audience to ask questions. The only requirement we make is that you share your questions with the rest of us. We have microphones at various locations. You'll have to come down and speak into a microphone so that all of us can hear you, unless you have a very, very loud voice. . .

Dr. Miller:
. . . or else I can repeat the question. I can probably hear you better. If anyone has questions, I will be very happy to field them.

From audience:
You imputed that there are those who prefer the page to the stage by citing the fact that Shakespeare wrote for the theatre and that is very true, but is it not possible that he never saw a stage production of his work that satisfied his literary nature?

Dr. Miller:
That's a very interesting question. The question is whether, in fact, it's a possibility that Shakespeare ever saw a production on the stage that satisfied his own imagination. No, I think it's very unlikely that he did, and there may be all sorts of reasons why it failed to. It may well be that it is in the nature of the literary imagination of an author that no work could ever by being visualized bring it to life in the way that he conceived it, for reasons which are very complicated and hard to do with mental imagery, I think. I don't want to go into this in too much detail, but I think that it is quite an interesting point and has a bearing on something which interests me very much about whether or not novels ought to be dramatized. I believe that the question of whether plays ought to be dramatized is a subset of the larger set of whether literature ought to be dramatized, and it has to do with the nature of mental images and how one imagines a work when one makes it. You see, I don't think that painters have a work imagined of which the canvas is simply a transcription of a phantom, pre-existent work which is in their head, nor do I believe that an author has a phantom version of King Lear in his head before he writes it and which is then transcribed onto the page of which, then, the performance is judged to be a deteriorated version. I think there's something very vague and odd that happens inside your head when you imagine the work and that there may be all sorts of very complicated reasons why someone like Shakespeare might have been dissatisfied with the performance, which is to do not with the fact that he imagined it differently or he imagined it more richly, but that he imagined it at all. By being imagined it probably makes it impossible that any performance could ever actually do justice to it because it is in the nature of the imagination not that it is richer than anything, but that the imagination has a curious sort of quality which is different logically, categorically from images which are

presented on a stage. When Shakespeare, if he did, as it were, feel dissatisfaction with something that he saw on the stage, it is not because it didn't come up to what he had imagined but that by being imagined at all, and by being performed at all, the two were discrepant from the very start, because it is in the nature of the imagination that no material representation of it can actually copy it. It has to do with all sorts of very peculiar aspects of mental imagery, such as the indeterminacy of its indeterminacy.

Let me just elucidate slightly what I mean by that. When we talk about the indeterminacy of a picture, it is determinately indeterminate. Let's think, for example, of a picture painted by Renoir with that particular sort of facture which leaves it quite undetermined how many buttons there are on a girl's coat as she walks in the Park Monceau. Now that is because there's something about the facture which makes it impossible to tell how many buttons. But it is quite determinate what makes it impossible to determine how many buttons because what is indeterminate about it is the facture. It is the blurriness of his painting which makes it impossible to tell how many buttons there are on her coat. Whereas when I dream of someone and cannot tell you how many buttons he had on his coat, it wasn't because I saw him blurrily because I don't dream blurrily. It wasn't because I visualized him blurrily. It's because my imagination is not like that. It can leave out how many buttons someone has on his coat without leaving a gap in the picture or without being blurred in any way. I think that if Shakespeare was, in fact, unsatisfied or perplexed or felt that the performance fell short, it might. I'd acknowledge that it might have fallen short for perfectly obvious, ordinary reasons, that they weren't very good that night or they weren't very good at all. But there is always a reason why I think it will fall short because it is a product of the imagination, and the imagination can never be reproduced in concrete physical reality. Someone who writes something is not transcribing the inside of his or her mind, and when someone paints something they're not painting a copy of the something inside their head. The dissatisfaction which any artist feels when they see something is not because their handiwork hasn't worked or the stage work hasn't worked, but because the two belong to different logical categories which in the end forbid transcription perfectly. Nevertheless, this goes a long way from the thrust of your question, the fact that there is such frustration and dissatisfaction on the part of an artist, is actually rather rare, I think. Although Chekhov had it on the first occasion of *The Seagull*, the second occasion of *The Seagull* he was delighted. It worked. When they did it in St. Petersburg it was a catastrophe. He thought it was horrible because it was underrehearsed. They did three days' rehearsal. When it was done by the Moscow Art Theatre by the Stanislavski and Ynorovich Danchenko Group, it was very attractive to him. There is no principle which will guarantee that something is going to be bad on the stage and better on the page. These people do intend their works for the stage. Chekhov intended his works when he wrote them as plays. He didn't intend his short stories to be seen on the stage, and I wonder what he would have thought about that. Now we do them as films. What would he have thought? I suspect he would have probably deplored them for reasons which I would like to go into in great detail and something for which I have a separate lecture. We obviously don't have time for that.

From audience:
Can anyone appreciate a play, or does it require a certain maturity of perception?

Dr. Miller:
I think that there are all sorts of different ways in which you can appreciate a play and like it and get something out of it and be intrigued by it. I think that there are certain sorts of plays where, in fact, it is not so much maturity of perception as an informed heart and an informed head. There are certain plays that you're not likely to get what's in them unless you know what went into them, and I think this is very much the case with Shakespeare. There are certain aspects of Shakespeare which, in fact, are the reason why he survived and is thought to be the greatest playwright of all, which has nothing whatever to do with what you as an audience know or might know. But, nevertheless, there are certain things which if you know or acquaint yourself with you will see more in them. I mean, I think, again, this question of a cognitive object, of what you see in a thing, is determined very much by what you know. The crudest examples of it are these experiments that are found in almost all first-year elementary psychology textbooks, the ones which you have a series of lines, and then there's a legend upside down which says "See the faces in the leaves," and quite suddenly you see faces. In other words, knowing some sort of thing that is required of you, you will see if something accommodates it; you will see those faces. Well, it is exactly the same, I think, with certain complicated works which depend on elaborate, emblematic, allegorical, and iconographic references. If you know, you will see them. If you don't, you won't see them, and it enriches the experience if you know that much more.

Now I know that this goes against the grain, I think, of a lot of modern, particularly democratic feelings in the community or in the universities, that something which depends on that much knowing goes against the grain of democracy, that it's elitist. It's wrong that an art which depends on knowing something—which, therefore, excludes those who don't know—is antidemocratic and, therefore, bad, and I think that's nonsense. I just think that you haven't got to use such inflammatory words as elitist in order to say this. Knowing things helps you to see things. But the great works always deliver a very large part of what is valuable in them without having to know very much other than your own heart.

From audience:
I have a question. I just recently completed a screen play. I'm not interested in the people who are interested in it. They keep sending it back wanting this to be altered to the point it really takes away from what I'm trying to get across. The agents that I want won't even let me in the door to read my script. Using your expertise, how can I get in that door?

Dr. Miller:

I don't know. I know nothing about screenwriting, and I know nothing really about the movie world at all. I've always walked rather fastidiously around the edges of the movie world because you have to have lunch with such impossible people.

From audience:

You should hear the requests I get, too.

Dr. Miller:

They are awful. In the old days, at least, they used to have a sort of picturesque, Neanderthal quality, which was really that they used to come shuffling out from the back of their cave, and you would hear rustling of straw. But now they're about eighteen and have cellular telephones, and I don't know how you impress or get round or penetrate their armor. I really don't know at all. Hollywood is a closed, exotic world to me, and I just don't know how you can do it. In a way, I think what you have to do is to forget Hollywood. There are independent filmmakers. I think you have to realize that if you're accepted by any of those studios or by that sort of money . . .

From audience:

I'm basically talking about literary agents.

Dr. Miller:

Oh, literary agents . . .

From audience:

. . . yes, right, who represent you.

Dr. Miller:

I don't know how people do that. I really don't. I've never understood how anyone starts at all. I really don't know.

From audience:

Think back; think back!

Dr. Miller:

Well, no, because I never started as a writer at all. I started as a performer. I was prepared to pull funny faces on a stage, and I did it at the university. One thing led to another, and now I'm lucky enough, having climbed up this back route. You get a name in one area, and you can actually interest people in another area. You see, if I say my name now to a literary agent, I can get in, although I wasn't primarily thought of as a literary person. I wish I could help. I mean, perhaps we can talk about it afterwards. I really don't have any practical advice to offer on that. It's very difficult.

From audience:
With regard to changes, scene changes, as it were, Fowler and then recently Marowitz—and I would like to hear what you have to say about that, particularly Marowitz.

Dr. Miller:
You mean actually changing text?

From audience:
Yes, so violently in that case.

Dr. Miller:
Well, I never quite know about that. I think it's one of the things that happens in art. You see, I actually do think that the history of art is partly, not altogether, but quite significantly, history of damage and injury and plagiarism and theft and robbery and violence of one sort or another, which doesn't matter to allographic works that continue to survive anyway. It matters when someone actually knocks the nose off an autographic work. If someone vandalizes the *Mona Lisa* or the *Pietà* in the Vatican it does matter, because the continued survival of the artifact is actually the only way in which it survives. I don't think it matters whatever Charles Marowitz does to a text because the text continues to live to be performed another day in its canonical or its complete version. I don't approve of them in the sense that it's not a version which I would like to see, but often they are very illuminating. I mean there are soft and greatly savage reconstructions of works. It doesn't bring them to life but it brings you to life in relationship to them. I think to declare them to be illegitimate is actually not in one's gift anyway. Anything goes. Everything wouldn't go if, in fact, Charles Marowitz were to say, "I'm going to do my version of *Hamlet* or *The Taming of the Shrew*, and just before I do, I'm going to destroy every text so that no one else can do it again." Then I think that would be vandalism. But there's no way in which you can do worse. The worst thing you can do is vandalize an evening.

From audience:
I'm interested in hearing you speculate about these concepts regarding the afterlife of a play in regards to oral discourse in general. It seems to me to be a rather easy and kind of logical transition that some of these things might hold for formal speaking events, public speeches, oratorical kinds of endeavors, etc. But if you can make that leap with me, and I don't know if you can, which for me is an easy one, what do these concepts have to say about human interaction, oral human interaction in general, about the kinds of dialogue that we share and exchange, not on the stage but in life?

Dr. Miller:
I think that's very interesting. I think it has connections really with the sort of work

that's going on a great deal now in experimental psychology, about the memorability of discourse and about what people remember people said and what people remember of who said what, in whose voice particular opinions were couched, who actually said that. It's amazing how inaccurate it is. Also the other thing which is very fascinating is how poor a record we have of what people actually said rather than the gist of what they said. Obviously what we get is we have a memory for gist and a very bad memory for the actual surface form of discourse, which, in a way, is what you'd expect. It's a much more economical system because what we want is gist. For most human business, gist is what you're after. Give me the gist! Give me the gist! I just want to know what it's about. I don't want to know whether he uh, ummed, what did he say? What is the gist? But memory for gist is very interesting business. If we, in fact, overstress gist, what we tend to do is lose the texture and character that actually gave discourse its distinctiveness. and in that sense I think this happens in plays. It goes back to what I was saying rather facetiously about *Long Day's Journey*. One of the things that I did when I did *Long Day's Journey* was to try and restore it, not to what O'Neill imagined, because I don't know what O'Neill imagined. As I said in answer to your question, sir, the nature of what someone's imagining is very ambiguous. But I wanted to restore it to the sort of conversation which I suspect he was referring to when he wrote the play, and that's a rather roundabout way of saying what he imagined. I imagined what he imagined was the conversations that he had heard as a child, and in that case it couldn't have possibly been like what he wrote if only for one reason that he wrote down things which, if repeated in the form that he wrote them down, couldn't possibly have been like the sound of what he heard in that people do not speak one after another. They do not speak in grammatical periods, punctuated in the way that he seems to have punctuated them. What I'm talking about really is the history or orthography, of what the process of literacy does to the recording of discourse, of how we actually memorize discourse when we write it down. In the case of Shakespeare, we're not really talking about that because we're talking about someone who wrote poetry, whose purpose was not recording how people talked, except in certain rapid, prosy parts of the plays where people are talking as I imagined he thought they were meant to be talking. But in the case of O'Neill, he is actually trying to record what he thinks he heard when he was a child or when he was a young man. We know from looking at it that it couldn't possibly be what he heard. It just doesn't look right. If you actually speak it out, it doesn't actually reproduce discourse that we know. One of the most important parts of it is that as we know from the psychology of turn-taking in conversations people interrupt, and as soon as people have heard what they think is the gist, they're already getting on with their gist, or else they are agreeing the other interlocutory into silence. What you get is someone's talking, and they say, "Yeah, yeah, um, um, yeah . . . ," and then they leap in. Now there isn't even a scintilla of a suspicion in the O'Neill text of all these interruptions and box shots and ungrammatical and ums and uhs and false starts and hanging clauses and sentences which fail to conclude and verbs which are not there, which are actually in the nature of real discourse. As a director what I had to do was to unravel the work back not to its gist, but to the work from which he as a writer had extracted its gist. What I believe O'Neill wrote down was, in a way, what the psychologists call a reversion to the real object. He had actually written what he thought the characters meant and then sprinkled on top of it the slang that he remembered as being characteristic slang of his particular period. But it is not the conversation of his period. People could not ever have talked like that. I hope this is in any way related to your question . . .

From audience:
In a strange way it is.

Dr. Miller:
I think that the plays are more and more concerned with a reproduction of ordinary discourse in a way that they weren't, say, at the time of Shakespeare, and certainly Restoration plays are highly artificial representations of talk. Modern plays, Mamet and Sam Shepard, and so forth, are much more given to actual discourse, and part of their pride and self-esteem is invested in the fact that they record talk as it was going on. Actually now I think in Mamet's plays they're written down to allow interruption, to actually guarantee it. Now the reason why this has happened, of course, is that we now write in the way that our predecessors never wrote. We write with benefit of the tape recorder, and the tape recorder has made a totally different business. I'm not saying that playwrights write with tape recorders, but they write with benefit of tape recorder. They have heard conversations for the first time. We don't hear conversations when we talk to one another. We hear the gist of our interlocutor. We hear what they mean. We don't hear what they say. It's a terribly important difference between hearing what someone means as opposed to hearing what someone says. It goes back to this question of copying and mimicking. When you copy someone, you actually copy the gist of what they're saying with one or two idioms. You very rarely copy how they said it. Tape recorders have made a great difference. It's actually made us hear conversations. We're startled now to hear how conversations sound on tape recorders, how actually unconcluded our sentences are. If I were to be forced to listen to my own talk, a form of torture which I think would make one begin to divulge information in a very short time, the thing that would be most agonizing to me would be the strange, ungrammatical hesitancies of my speech, something which I wouldn't have had to suffer fifty years ago. The tape recorders made the audibility of human speech different from the reproducibility of discourse, totally different. That's all to the nature of discourse.

From audience:
Thank you. You continue to raise more questions, but there are other people here.

From audience:
You speak in the defense of artists as mutators, but in your viewing of American productions of Shakespeare in the director's attempts to make Shakespeare palatable to an American audience, are there any typical traps or problems that arise? Is there anything that bothers you in the modernization or Americanization or the American mutations of Shakespeare?

Dr. Miller:
I should say that when I talk about the mutations that are introduced, I never really introduce them for the purpose of making the plays palatable to an audience. That's not the name of the game. I play with plays because they divert me; they interest me a great deal. I like playing with them, and you have to remember the curious force of that word "play." The fact that the object upon which we go to work is called play is not to be overlooked. The fluid mode of this enterprise is, in fact, part of what makes it attractive both to us who perform in it and for the audience. We play around with it because it's diverting to do so, not because we are trying to make it relevant or palatable. It is hoped to be hoped by those who, in fact, indulge in it, that when they actually exercise their playful imagination it will become palatable to an audience. When you play with Shakespeare it will divert an audience. But I'm not trying to do that. There are pitfalls. I think the pitfalls are when you deliberately try to take Shakespeare and say, look, they won't understand him unless he's in modern dress. I don't believe that there is a particular virtue about doing him in modern dress, nor do I think it is a particular vice to do it in modern dress. You do one thing or the other. The name of the game is not relevance or attractiveness. Some effort must be made by any audience to see these works as being products of the past. That's actually one of the things that makes them attractive. We visit them for the purpose of doing what Henry James talked about, visiting the unvisitable past, of recognizing the extent to which, as L. B. Hartley said, the past is foreign country where they do things differently. If we insist always on dressing them in suits or Americanizing them, or doing something which brings them closer to our lives as being the only way in which we can, as it were, tolerate them, then I think it's very foolish. It's really an example of what T. S. Eliot refers to as overvaluing our own times, believing that where we live is the center. It's not. We don't inhabit the metropolis of history. We're in the suburbs.

Dean Cobble:
Our time is getting on. Our long day's journey may even be a bit later in the night. I want to thank again Jonathan Miller for being here with us and sharing his thoughts and contributing mightily to our university experience and we'll stand adjourned. Thank you.

Jonathan Miller was born in 1934 in London and educated at St. Paul's School. He read natural sciences at St. John's College, Cambridge, and qualified as a Doctor of Medicine at University College, London, in 1959.

Dr. Miller co-authored and appeared in *Beyond The Fringe* both in London and New York from 1961 to 1964. After several successful BBC television films, he turned his attention to Shakespeare productions for the National Theater (including his highly acclaimed staging of *The Merchant of Venice* with Sir Laurence Olivier and Joan Plowright), Greenwich Theater (*All's Well That End's Well, Hamlet,* and *Measure for Measure*), and the Oxford and Cambridge Shakespeare Company (*Twelfth Night, Hamlet,* and *Julius Caesar*). Among the non-Shakespearean plays he has directed are *Danton's Death, Ghosts,* Beaumarchais' *The Marriage of Figaro, The Seagull,* and a *Three Sisters* that particularly distinguished throughout its run, on tour and in the West End. In 1979, he directed a new production of *A Midsummer Night's Dream* for the Vienna Burgtheater.

Jonathan Miller made his operatic directing debut in 1973 with the British premiere of *Arden Must Die* by Alexander Goehn. Since then, he has directed *Cosi Fan Tutte, Rigoletto, Orfeo,* and *Eugene Onegin* for the Kent Opera; during 1978-79, his much-praised production of *Orfeo* also played at nearly every major English festival. He directed Janacek's *The Cunning Little Vixen* for Glyndebourne in 1975 (revived 1977), and also for the Australian Opera and Frankfurt Opera. In November of 1978, he made his directorial debut at the English National Opera with a new and highly original production of *The Marriage of Figaro*; other operatic works in the 1978-79 season included *The Flying Dutchman* for Frankfurt Opera, and a new production of *La Traviata* for Kent Opera at the 1979 Edinburgh Festival, collaborating with the English National Opera in his capacity as Associate Producer comprises one production yearly — in 1980, *Arabella*; in 1981, *Othello*; in 1982, *Rigoletto*. For Kent Opera, he directed *Falstaff* in 1980 and Fidelio in 1982. In June, 1982, Dr. Miller directed *Cosi Fan Tutte* for the Opera Theater of St. Louis.

In 1977, he gave the T.S. Eliot memorial lectures at Kent University and in 1984 the Clark lectures at Cambridge.

Jonathan Miller's series on the history of medicine, *The Body in Question*, for BBC-TV brought him to the American public. In 1983, he conducted 15 interviews for BBC-TV on the foundations of psychology. Between 1980 and 1982, he produced 12 plays for the BBC's Shakespeare series, directing six of them.

Dr. Miller is also the author of the bestsellers *The Human Body* and *The Facts of Life* (pop-up books) as well as *States of Mind.* His most recent work, *Subsequent Performances*, discusses the "afterlife" of a dramatic work of art, a director's rights and responsibilities in presenting a classic work when the passage of time begins to impose awkward problems of re-creation and interpretation.

For two years Dr. Miller worked at the University of Sussex in the field of cognitive psychology. He returned to the arts in the 1985-86 season, directing productions of *Cosi Fan Tutte* for the BBC, and *Don Giovanni* and *The Magic Flute* for the English National Opera.

In 1986, Dr. Miller directed *Long Day's Journey into Night* on Broadway for which he received a Tony nomination. From 1987 to 1990, Jonathan Miller was the Artistic Director of the Old Vic. In February 1991, he made his New York metropolitan Opera debut with his production of Janacek's *Katya Kabanova*, an opera not performed in the United States for over 70 years. Earlier in this year, he directed *La Fanciulla del West* at La Scala in Milan, Italy. Late in 1991, Dr. Miller will mount his productions of *The Marriage of Figaro* in Venice and *Cosi Fan Tutte* at the May Festival in Florence.

Jonathan Miller is an Honorary Fellow of the Royal Academy, an Albert Medalist for the Royal Society of the Arts. In recent months, he finished two more television series, one on madness, and the other called *Born Talking* on language, talk and conversation.

STATE PRODUCTIONS

1962	UNDER PLAIN COVER (Royal Court Theatre)
1964	THE OLD GLORY (American Place Theater, New York)
1966	COME LIVE WITH ME (New Haven, Conn.)
1967	BENITO CERENO (Yale University)
1967	PROMETHEUS BOUND (Yale University)
1968	BENITO CERENO (Mermaid Theatre)
1968	SCHOOL FOR SCANDAL (Nottingham Playhouse)
1969	THE SEAGULL (Nottingham Playhouse)
1969	KING LEAR (Nottingham Playhouse)
1970	HAMLET (Arts Theatre, Cambridge)
1970	THE TEMPEST (Mermaid Theatre)
1970	KING LEAR (National Theatre, Old Vic)
1970	THE MERCHANT OF VENICE (National Theatre, Old Vic; a TV production, 1973)
1971	PROMETHEUS BOUND (National Theatre, Old Vic)
1971	DANTON'S DEATH (National Theatre, Old Vic)
1972	SCHOOL FOR SCANDAL (National Theatre, Old Vic)
1972	THE TAMING OF THE SHREW (Chichester)

1973	THE MALCONTENT (Nottingham Playhouse)
1973	THE SEAGULL (Chichester)
1974	MEASURE FOR MEASURE (National Theatre, Old Vic)
1974	THE MARRIAGE OF FIGARO (National Theatre, Old Vic)
1974	THE FREEWAY (National Theatre, Old Vic)
1974	FAMILY ROMANCES: GHOSTS; THE SEAGULL; HAMLET (Greenwich Theatre)
1974	ARDEN MUST DIE (Sadler's Wells Theatre)
1975	THE IMPORTANCE OF BEING EARNEST (Greenwich Theatre)
1975	ALL'S WELL THAT ENDS WELL (Greenwich Theatre)
1975	COSI FAN TUTTE (Kent Opera)
1975	RIGOLETTO (Kent Opera)
1975	THE CUNNING LITTLE VIXEN (Glyndebourne; revived 1977)
1976	LA FAVOLA D'ORFEO (Kent Opera; BBC TV presentation, 1979)
1976	PLEASURE AT HER MAJESTY'S (Amnesty benefit, Her Majesty's Theatre filmed by Roger Graef)
1976	THE THREE SISTERS (Cambridge)
1977	EUGENE ONEGIN (Kent Opera)
1978	THE MARRIAGE OF FIGARO (English National Opera)
1979	LA TRAVIATA (Kent Opera)
1979	SHE WOULD IF SHE COULD (Greenwich Theatre)
1979	THE FLYING DUTCHMAN (Frankfurt)
1979	THE TURN OF THE SCREW (English National Opera)
1980	ARABELLA (English National Opera)
1980-1	FALSTAFF (Kent Opera)
1981	OTHELLO (English National Opera)
1982	RIGOLETTO (English National Opera; Thames TV Production, 1983)
1982	COSI FAN TUTTE (St. Louis, Missouri)
1982	HAMLET (Donmar Warehouse)
1982-3	FIDELIO (Kent Opera)
1983	THE MAGIC FLUTE (Scottish Opera)
1985	DON GIOVANNI (English National Opera)

FILM AND TELEVISION

1962-3	WHAT'S GOING ON NOW (TV series, New York) director
1964	ONE WAY PENDULUM (Woodfall Films, dir. Peter Yates) actor
1964-5	MONITOR (BBC TV) series editor/presenter
1965	PROFILES IN COURAGE: ANNE HUTCHINSON (TV New York, dir. José Quintero) writer
1965	THE DRINKING PARTY (Plato's Symposium) (BBC TV 'Sunday Night' film) producer-director
1966	ALICE IN WONDERLAND (BBC TV film) producer-director
1967	SCOTCH (documentary film for John Walker & Sons) writer-director

1968	OH WHISTLE AND I'LL COME TO YOU (BBC TV 'Omnibus' film) producer-director
1970	TAKE A GIRL LIKE YOU (Columbia Pictures) director
1973	CLAY (BBC TV 'Full House' film) director
1980	THE MERCHANT OF VENICE (The BBC Television Shakespeare, dir. Jack Gold) producer
1980	ALL'S WELL THAT ENDS WELL (BBC Television Shakespeare, dir. Elija Moshinsky) producer
1980	A WINTER'S TALE (BBC Television Shakespeare, dir. Jane Howell) producer
1980	ANTONY AND CLEOPATRA (BBC Television Shakespeare) producer-director
1981	TIMON OF ATHENS (BBC Television Shakespeare) producer-director
1981	OTHELLO (BBC Television Shakespeare) producer-director
1981	TROILUS AND CRESSIDA (BBC Television Shakespeare) producer-director
1981	A MIDSUMMER NIGHT'S DREAM (BBC Television Shakespeare, dir., Elija Moshinsky) producer
1981	HENRY VI: PARTS I-III (BBC Television Shakespeare, dir. Jane Howell) producer
1982	KING LEAR (BBC Television Shakespeare) director
1982	STATES OF MIND (BBC TV, 15-part series) writer-presenter
1983	RIGOLETTO (Thames TV/Channel 4) introduced/collaborated on TV version of English National Opera production
1984	THE BEGGAR'S OPERA (BBC TV) producer-director
1984	IVAN (BBC TV 'Horizon' documentary, with Ivan Vaughan and Jonathan Miller) presenter
1985	COSI FAN TUTTE (BBC TV) director